Metal Toys

Metal Toys

JUDITH MILLER

LONDON, NEW YORK,
MUNICH, MELBOURNE, DELHI

A joint production from DK and THE PRICE GUIDE COMPANY

DK DELHI

Designer Malavika Talukder
Editors Larissa Sayers **DTP** Pankaj Sharma
Cutouts Harish Aggarwal, Pushpak Tyagi
Managing Art Editor Aparna Sharma

DK LONDON

Editor Katie John **Designers** Lee Riches, Katie Eke
DTP, Reproduction, and Design Adam Walker
Production Elizabeth Warman
Managing Art Editor Heather McCarry

THE PRICE GUIDE COMPANY LIMITED

Publishing Manager Julie Brooke   **Editor** Dan Dunlavey
Editorial Assistants Jessica Bishop and Sandra Lange
Digital Image Co-ordinator Ellen Sinclair

While every care has been taken in the compilation of this guide, neither the authors nor the publishers accept any
liability for any financial or other loss incurred by reliance placed on the information contained in *Metal Toys*.

First published in the USA in 2006 by DK Publishing, Inc.
375 Hudson Street, New York, NY 10014

First published in Great Britain in 2006 by Dorling Kindersley Limited,
80 Strand, London WC2R 0RL
A Penguin Company

The Price Guide Company (UK) Ltd: info@thepriceguidecompany.com

2 4 6 8 10 9 7 5 3 1

CIP catalog records for this book are available from the Library of Congress and the British Library.

UK ISBN-13: 978 1 4053 0624 9
UK ISBN-10: 1 4053 0624 6

US ISBN-13: 978-0-7566-1921-3
US ISBN-10: 0-7566-1921-1

Proofing by MDP, UK
Printed in China by Hung Hing Offset Printing Company Ltd

Discover more at
www.dk.com

CONTENTS

INTRODUCTION

While reading this book, many of you may have cause to regret having
played quite so enthusiastically with your toy cars, planes, and boats in
your childhood years. It is only once our toys bear the scars of playground
wear and have long since been separated from their boxes that most of us
realize the value of keeping them in pristine condition. However, you can't
put a price on fun, and the reason these toys appeal to so many collectors
is precisely because they are evocative of our more innocent years. From
19th-century penny toys to the latest incarnation of the Batmobile, these
models have fired the imaginations of generations of children and continue
to appeal to enthusiasts across the globe. I'm sure your inner child will be
delighted by the selection of toys on the following pages.

Judith Miller

Star Ratings

Each of the toys in this book has a star rating according to its value: .

★ $10–200; £5–100 ★★ $200–500; £100–250 ★★★ $500–1,000; £250–500
★★★★ $1,000–2,000; £500–1,000 ★★★★★ $2,000 upward; £1,000 upward

SHEET METAL

Until the mid-19th century, most toy vehicles had been made from wood and card. Sheet metal was more resilient and could be manipulated more cheaply and efficiently than wood using new factory technology. Metal could also be run through a printing press, providing an economical way of applying bright decoration to toys. The age of mass-produced toys had arrived.

German manufacturers such as Bing, Günthermann, and Märklin dominated the industry in the early days until the outbreak of war in 1914 isolated them from international markets, allowing companies in France, England, and America to flourish. The American industry, centered around Connecticut, survived the Depression thanks in part to the low cost of tinplate toys. Japan was home to dozens of successful tinplate toy makers, achieving particular success between the late 1940s and early 1960s.

SHEET METAL

DETAIL: Lithograph of windscreen wipers, steering wheel, and driver.

ARNOLD

Arnold sheet metal Gescha Auto Fox Porsche, with ruby lacquer and printed decoration; marked "Auto Fox Nr. 559." *1950s* ★ ☆ ☆ ☆ ☆

SHEET METAL

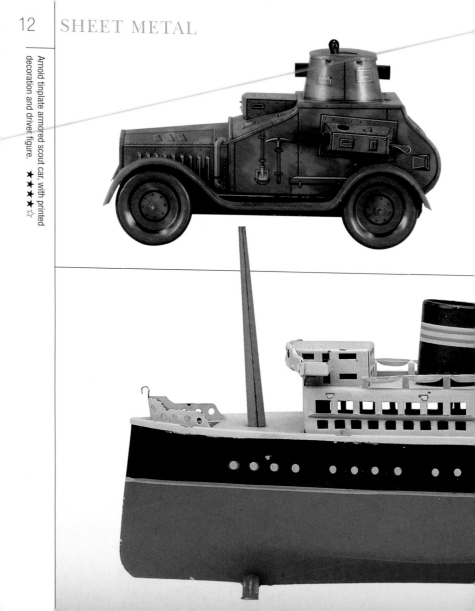

Arnold tinplate armored scout car, with printed decoration and driver figure. ★★★★☆

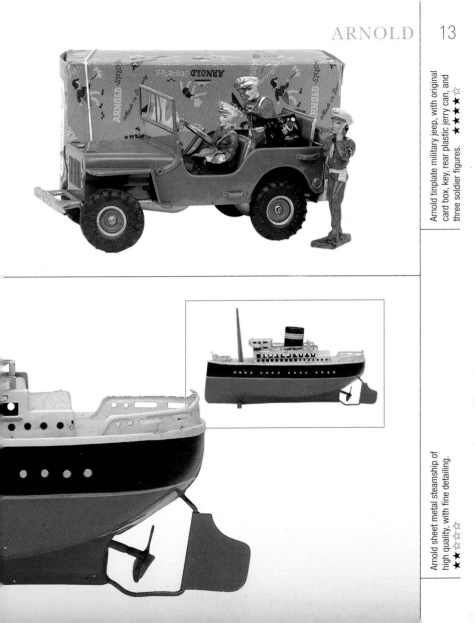

Arnold tinplate military jeep, with original card box, key, rear plastic jerry can, and three soldier figures. ★ ★ ★ ☆

Arnold sheet metal steamship of high quality, with fine detailing. ★ ★ ☆ ☆ ☆

Arnold tinplate delivery van in German Post Office livery; has opening rear door and friction drive mechanism. ★★★☆☆

Arnold tinplate MAN diesel breakdown lorry; has friction drive mechanism and black jib with hook and chain. ★★★☆☆

Arnold tinplate lorry-mounted crane, with friction drive mechanism; also has original box and instructions slip. ★★★☆☆

Arnold tinplate Express container truck, with friction drive mechanism and detachable container; rare variation. ★★★☆☆

DETAIL: Model with original instruction sheet.

MAC *700*

zeigt Dir seine Fahrkunst:

...d läuft im Leerlauf, Fahrer **A₂B₂**
...zen

...d läuft im Leerlauf, Fahrer **A₁B₂**
...auf und ab

...d fährt im Kreis, Fahrer hält **A₁B₁**
...rt ab, steigt wieder auf und
...ter

...d fährt im Kreis und Fahrer **A₂B₁**
...zen

Here is how to run it:

...cycle standing, clockwork **A₂B₂**
...g, Mac remains sitting,

...cycle standing, clockwork- **A₁B₂**,
...g, Mac gets off, stands beside
...torcycle, and gets on it again,

...rcycle drives in circles, stops, **A₁B₁**
...gets off, stands beside the
...rcycle, gets on it again, then
...on driving,

...e drives in circles, Mac **A₂B₁**

ARNOLD

Karl Arnold established his successful family business in Nuremberg, the center of Germany's metal toy industry, in 1906. Arnold toys from this period can be difficult to identify as they were not marked, but the ships and doll's house accessories, in particular, are worth seeking out due to a reputation for high quality.

Bombing during the Second World War destroyed the entire operation, although the firm did eventually recover. In the years immediately following the war, Nuremberg came under American control; for this reason, many toys from this period are stamped "Made in US Zone Germany." Under Karl's son, Ernst, Arnold prospered once again in the 1950s, exporting tin toys worldwide; the company's clockwork "Mac 700" motorcycle was among the most popular toys of its day. During the 1960s, Arnold abandoned tin toys altogether to concentrate on the "Rapido" range of model railways.

Arnold tinplate "Mac 700" clockwork motorcycle, with original key and instruction sheet. Rider figure mechanically mounts and dismounts. *c.1945* ★ ★ ☆ ☆ ☆

Arnold tinplate container lorry, with friction drive mechanism and detachable tank container; scarce variation. ★★★☆☆

Features of this truck include red and white chevrons to the front of the cab, high sides, and a drop-down tailgate.

Arnold tinplate long-wheelbase DAF truck, with friction drive mechanism; comes with original box. ★★★☆☆

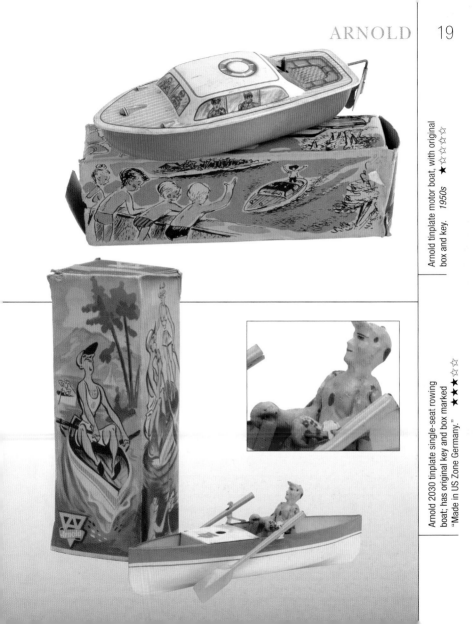

Arnold tinplate motor boat, with original box and key. *1950s* ★ ☆☆☆☆

Arnold 2030 tinplate single-seat rowing boat; has original key and box marked "Made in US Zone Germany." ★★★☆

Like many older tinplate toys, this ship has been painted by hand.

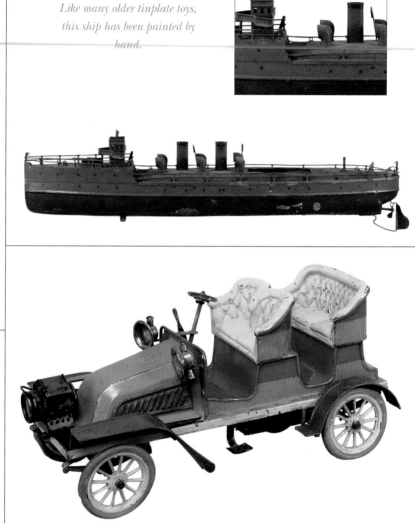

Bing tinplate amphibious aircraft: hand-painted, with clockwork mechanism. Early aeronautical toy. ★★★★☆

The features of this finely modeled boat include a full canopy and railed sides.

Bing tinplate river boat: hand-painted, with clockwork mechanism. ★★★★

Bing steam-driven tinplate and diecast road roller,
with detachable smoke stack and burner tray.
Has original box. ★★★☆☆

Distler Electro Matic tinplate Porsche 356,
with battery-operated mechanism. Has
original box. *1950s* ★★★☆☆

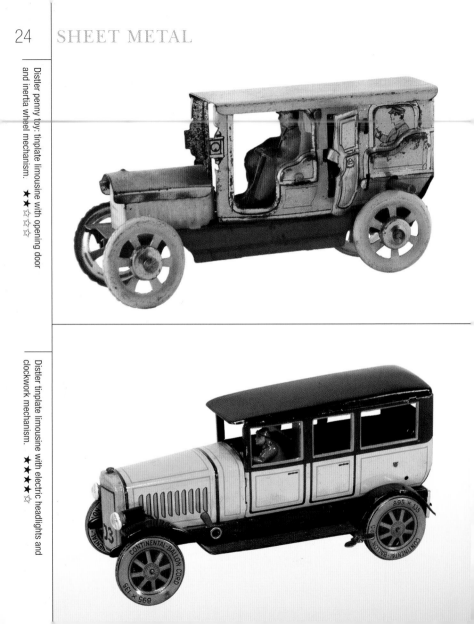

Distler penny toy: tinplate limousine with opening door and inertia wheel mechanism. ★★☆☆☆

Distler tinplate limousine with electric headlights and clockwork mechanism. ★★★★☆

Distler tinplate open-style fire engine, with escape
ladder and clockwork mechanism. ★ ★ ★ ☆ ☆

Distler 5881 tinplate Dapolin truck, with driver figure
and electrical lighting and movement. ★ ★ ★ ★ ★

Günthermann tinplate "Vis-à-Vis" clockwork auto, so-called because the riders sit face to face. ★★★★ ★★

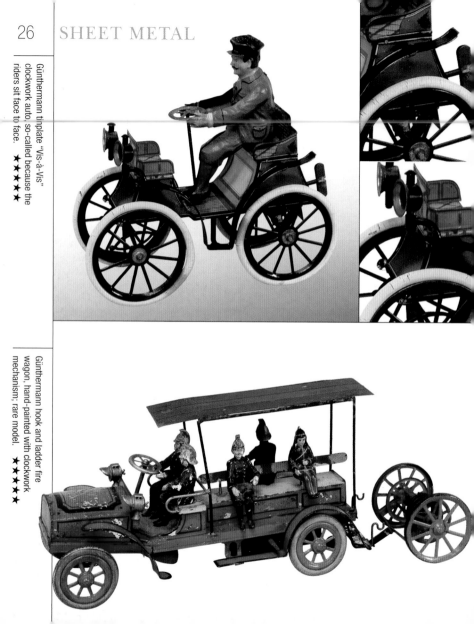

Günthermann hook and ladder fire wagon, hand-painted with clockwork mechanism; rare model. ★★★★ ★★

Günthermann tinplate double-decker
bus, with advertising boards on sides and
clockwork mechanism. ★★★☆

Günthermann 1069 sheet metal water
plane, with printed decoration and moving
propeller. ★★★☆☆

FIRE ENGINES

p.150

p.187

p.122

p.211

p.186

p.200

p.124

p.191

p.26

p.123

p.123

FIRE ENGINES

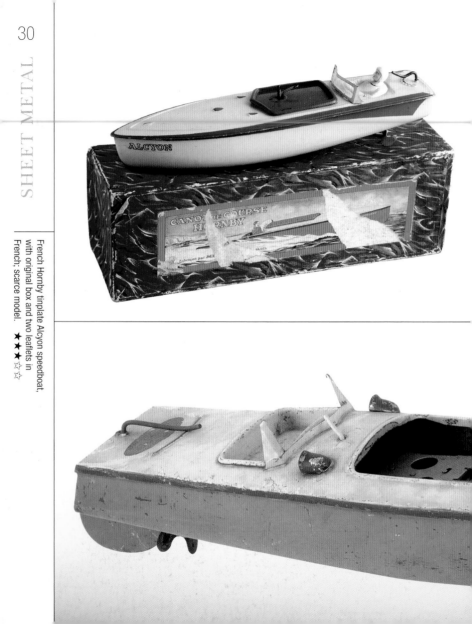

French Hornby tinplate Alcyon speedboat, with original box and two leaflets in French; scarce model. ★★★☆☆

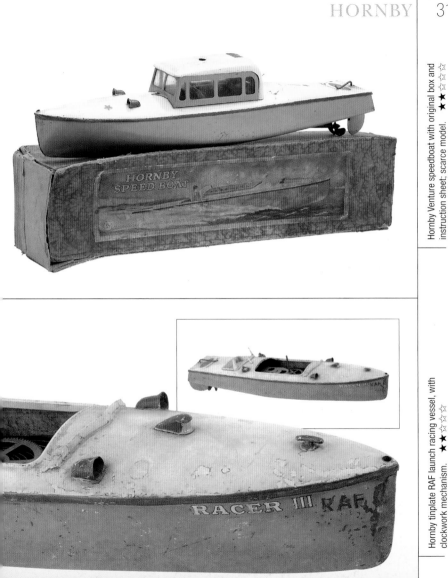

Hornby Venture speedboat with original box and instruction sheet; scarce model. ★ ☆ ☆ ☆

Hornby tinplate RAF launch racing vessel, with clockwork mechanism. ★ ★ ☆ ☆

Yonezawa tinplate taxi, with battery-operated "mystery action," has original box. *1960s* ★ ☆☆☆☆

Alps tinplate Mercedes 230SL, with battery-powered mechanism; has original box. ★ ★ ☆ ☆

EXPORT TOYS

The Japanese tinplate toy business dates back to the turn of the 19th century, but it was not until after the Second World War that production really boomed. Toys from the late 1940s marked "Occupied Japan" or "OJ" (referring to the US occupation of Japan at the time) sometimes carry a premium and appeal to collectors who specialize in this area. Companies such as Marusan, Bandai, and Yonezawa prospered by catering to the almost insatiable American appetite for tin toys.

Even after the end of the occupation, Japanese toymakers continued to draw inspiration from American marques such as Chevrolet and Lincoln, and produced tin versions of New York cabs and Greyhound buses. Toward the end of the 1960s, tin was phased out in favor of less expensive materials. The highest-quality Japanese tinplate toys are revered by many collectors as some of the finest ever made.

Hadson tinplate Greyhound bus, with clockwork mechansm. ★★★☆☆

Yonezawa tinplate MG roadster, with inertia drive mechanism. ★☆☆☆☆

Japanese tinplate tank, with clockwork
mechanism and bright camouflage-style
decoration. *1930s* ★☆☆☆☆

Modern Toys tinplate tank, with
clockwork mechanism; marked with
star and "M-05." ★ ☆ ☆ ☆ ☆

Japanese tinplate BMW Isetta bubble car, with clockwork mechanism. ★ ★ ☆ ☆ ☆

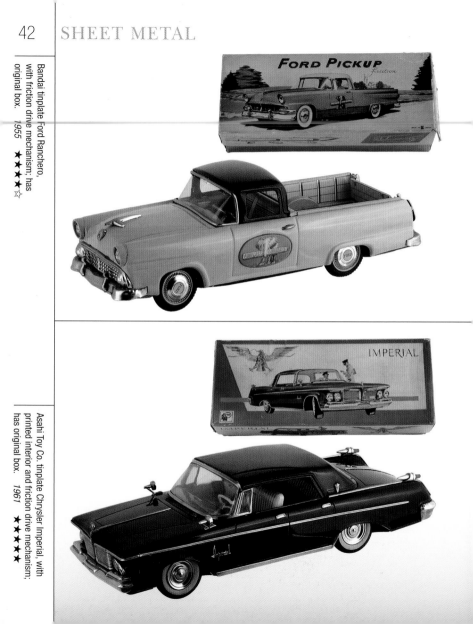

Bandai tinplate Ford Ranchero, with friction drive mechanism; has original box. *1955* ★★★★☆

Asahi Toy Co. tinplate Chrysler Imperial, with printed interior and friction drive mechanism; has original box. *1961* ★★★★★

SSS tinplate Fleetwood Cadillac, with rubber tires and friction drive mechanism; has original box.   *1961*   ★★★★★

Modern Toys tinplate Lincoln, with friction drive mechanism and siren sounds; has original box.   *1957*   ★★★★★

Marusan tinplate Chevrolet, with colorful printed interior and friction drive mechanism; has original box. *1954* ★★★★★★

Marusan tinplate Cadillac, with battery-operated mechanism and electric lights; has original box. *1953* ★★★★★

Line Mar Toys tinplate Lincoln Mark II Continental, with friction drive mechanism; has original box. ★★★★

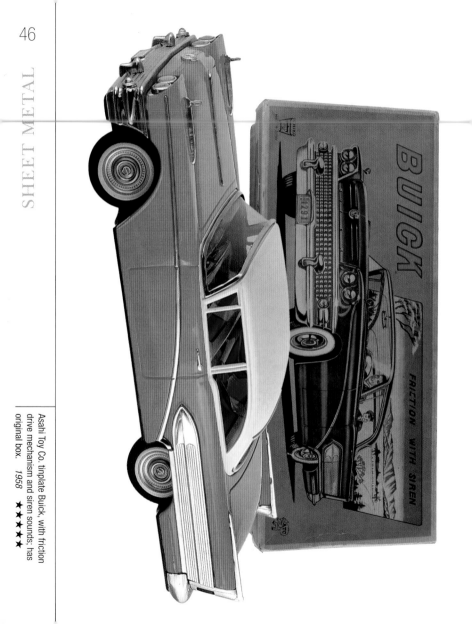

Asahi Toy Co. tinplate Buick, with friction drive mechanism and siren sounds; has original box. *1958* ★★★★★

Yonezawa tinplate Electro Toy racer, with battery-operated mechanism; has original box. ★★★★

BATTERY
OPERATED

SUPER PATRO

N
LIT

HIGHWAY PATROL

POLICE PATROL

DETAIL: Picture on box, featuring siren and flashing light.

MYSTERY ACTION

In an attempt to make their toys stand out from the crowd, some Japanese manufacturers added battery-operated novelty features to their products. Many of these were billed as "Mystery Action" on the toy's box, often with an awkwardly phrased description. Although the more outlandish mechanisms were reserved for space toys, cars and trucks were also advertized with "Mystery Action." The most common movement was similar to that used by Schuco's "Turning Car," which steered the vehicle in random directions. Others featured actions varying from flashing lights and siren noises to truly idiosyncratic devices; for example, Marusan's "Smoky Joe" car featured a driver with an outsize head, who puffed on a smoking pipe.

Masudaya tinplate "Super Patrol-Man" with battery-operated "mystery action," including light and siren. ★★☆☆☆

Usagiya tinplate "Rabbit" motorcycle and sidecar,
with friction drive mechanism; scarce model.
Has original box.   *1950s*   ★★★
★★☆☆

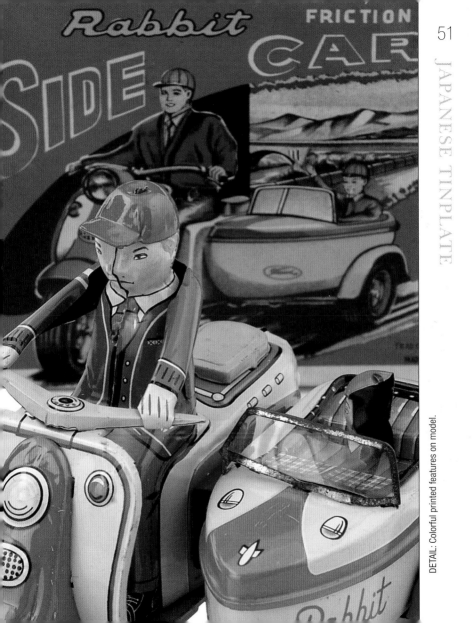

DETAIL: Colorful printed features on model.

SMOKY JOE

MYSTERY ACTION DRIVE · FANCY MOBILE

Marusan tinplate "Smoky Joe" car, with battery-operated "mystery action" of driver smoking a pipe. Has original box. ★★☆☆☆

Japanese tinplate San Francisco cable car, with friction drive mechanism. Has original box. ☆☆☆☆ ★

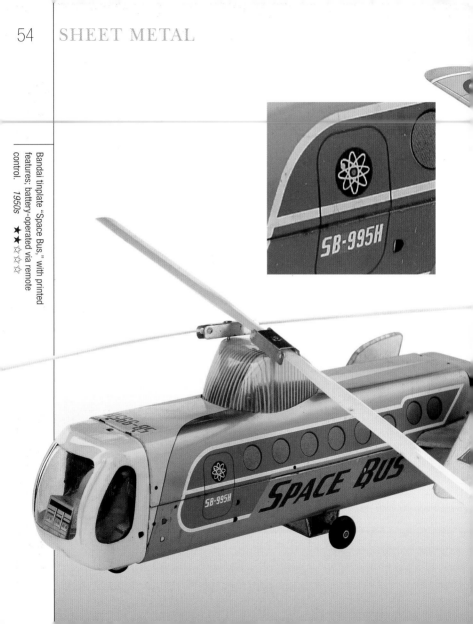

Bandai tinplate "Space Bus," with printed features; battery-operated via remote control. *1950s* ★★☆☆☆

Straco Bristol Bulldog aircraft, with pressed tin radial engine and battery-powered mechanism. *Late 1950s* ★ ☆☆☆☆

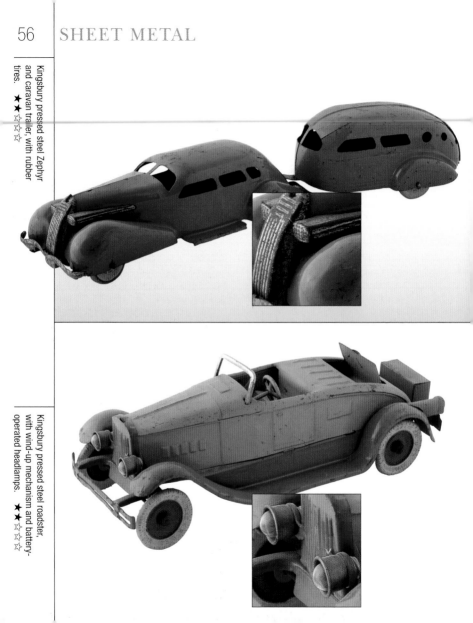

Kingsbury pressed steel Zephyr and caravan trailer, with rubber tires. ★★☆☆☆

Kingsbury pressed steel roadster, with wind-up mechanism and battery-operated headlamps. ★★☆☆☆

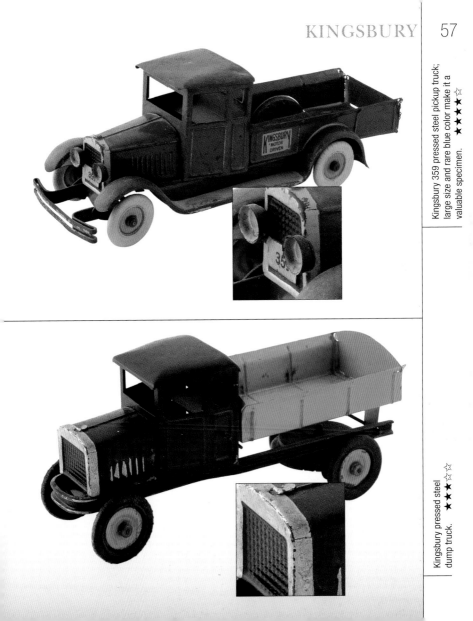

Kingsbury 359 pressed steel pickup truck; large size and rare blue color make it a valuable specimen. ★★★★☆

Kingsbury pressed steel dump truck. ★★☆☆

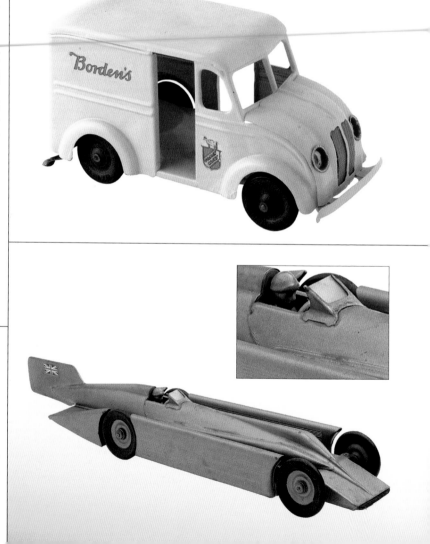

Kingsbury pressed steel Divco dairy truck, with wind-up mechanism. ★★★☆☆

Kingsbury pressed metal model of the record-breaking Golden Arrow land speed car, with driver figure. ★★★★☆

Märklin Constructor 1151 tinplate low-wing monoplane, with original box and instruction manual. ★★★☆☆

"To be able to fill leisure intelligently is the last product of civilization."

ARNOLD J. TOYNBEE, HISTORIAN

Märklin 127 D-LZ zeppelin: this large, early hand-painted example, complete with box, is especially valuable. ★★★★★

Märklin 1006 sheet metal tank lorry, with doors and tank that open; also has original box, instructions, and accessories. *c.1930* ★★★★★

DETAIL.: Front view, with "1101" registration.

Märklin Constructor Mercedes Benz racing car, with racing number "1," has clockwork mechanism. ★★★★☆

Märklin Constructor truck, with rubber tires and clockwork mechanism; rare model. *1930* ★★ ★★★★

Märklin limousine, with opening doors and clockwork mechanism; one of Märklin's finest models. ★★★★★

DETAIL: Decoration on Dipsy Car.

MARX

The Marx Toys empire was founded by brothers Louis and David Marx in 1919. In its first two years, the firm distributed the products of other companies, but it soon grew to become the largest toy manufacturer in the world. The Marx range of tinplate vehicles was extensive, encompassing everything from carts to zeppelins; a high-profile partnership with Disney helped the firm find more customers. Louis Marx was even pictured on the cover of *Time* magazine in 1955, with the title "The Toy King."

Rapid overseas expansion saw Marx factories open in Wales and France. After the 1950s, fewer tinplate toys were made as production switched to cheaper synthetic materials. Early Marx toys are eagerly sought after by collectors and often fetch very high prices.

Marx tinplate and celluloid Disney Dipsy Car, driven by Donald Duck, with wind-up mechanism; has original box. ★★★☆☆

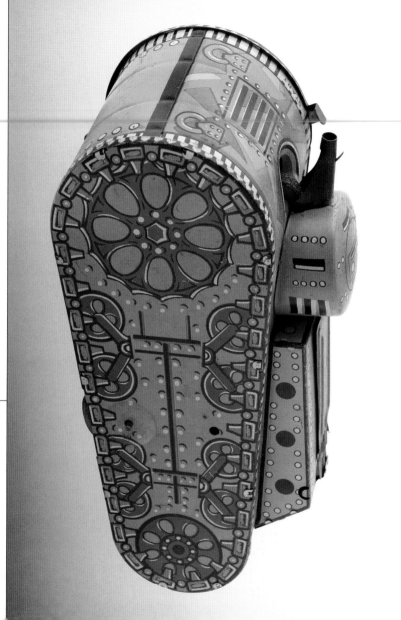

Marx tinplate Doughboy tank, with clockwork mechanism and interior figure that moves up and down. ★★☆☆☆

Marx tinplate "Hee Haw" Balky Mule cart, with wind-up action. ★ ★ ☆ ☆

Marx tinplate "Old Jalopy" limousine, with clockwork mechanism. *1930s* ★ ☆ ☆ ☆

Marx tinplate racer, with printed decoration and driver figure; has clockwork mechanism. ★★★☆☆

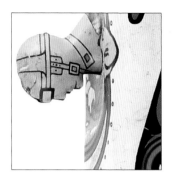

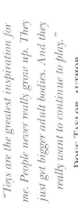

"Toys are the greatest inspiration for me. People never really grow up. They just get bigger adult bodies. And they really want to continue to play."

DOUG TAYLOR, AUTHOR

Marx tinplate racer, with single seat and driver figure; has clockwork mechanism. *1950s* ★★★☆☆

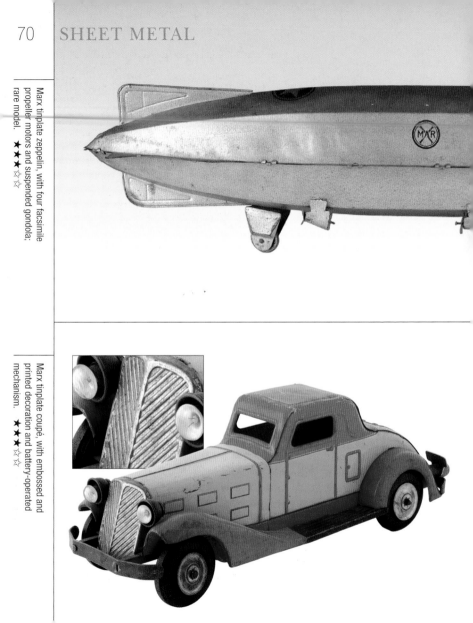

Marx tinplate zeppelin, with four facsimile propeller motors and suspended gondola; rare model. ★★★★☆☆

Marx tinplate coupé, with embossed and printed decoration and battery-operated mechanism. ★★★★☆☆

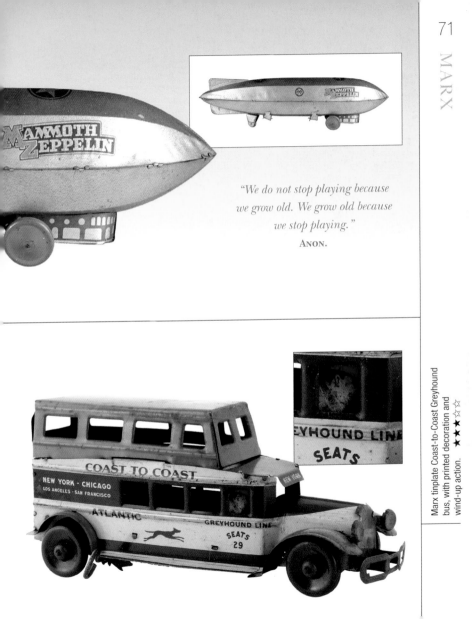

MAMMOTH ZEPPELIN

"We do not stop playing because
we grow old. We grow old because
we stop playing."

ANON.

COAST TO COAST

NEW YORK · CHICAGO
LOS ANGELES · SAN FRANCISCO

ATLANTIC

GREYHOUND LINE

SEATS
29

GREYHOUND LINE

SEATS

Marx tinplate Coast-to-Coast Greyhound
bus, with printed decoration and
wind-up action. ★ ★ ★ ☆ ☆

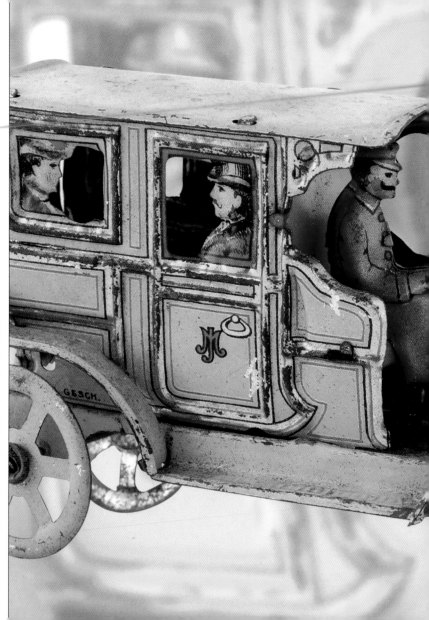

DETAIL: Fine decorative detail on the limousine and figures.

PENNY TOYS

Among the earliest metal toys were the very basic and inexpensive tinplate "Penny Toys," constructed from sheet metal cut-outs held together with folded tabs. They were imported in vast quantities from Germany and Japan from the late 1800s onwards to be sold by street traders, peddlers, and toy arcades.

The most popular designs included bugs, rattles, and tops, but the onset of the First World War in 1914 created a demand for military toys. The excitement surrounding the new discipline of aviation and the importance of naval power were reflected in the popularity of aircraft and boats. Toy cars were not as widespread, although several firms did create tin limousines and omnibuses. Penny toys were the only toys available to children from poorer families, and they sold very well.

Meier tinplate limousine penny toy with fine detailing, including driver and passengers. ☆☆☆ ★★★ ★★

Meier tinplate "Meteor Boat" penny toy, with candy container, sliding cover on deck, and inertia drive wheel.
★ ★ ★ ☆ ☆

Meier tinplate coach penny toy, with embossed and printed decoration.
★ ★ ☆ ☆ ☆

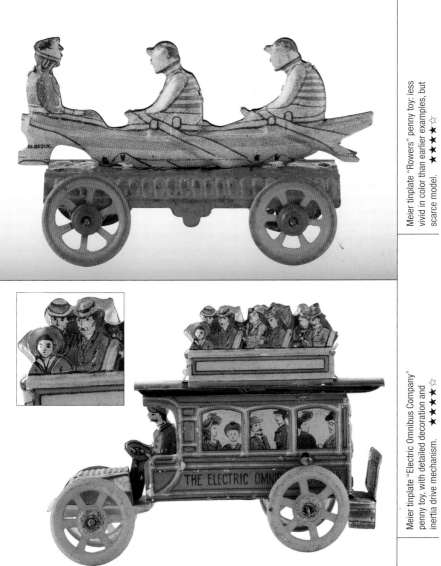

Meier tinplate "Rowers" penny toy: less vivid in color than earlier examples, but scarce model. ★★★☆

Meier tinplate "Electric Omnibus Company" penny toy, with detailed decoration and inertia drive mechanism. ★★★★☆

Meier tinplate horse-drawn dray penny toy, with embossed and printed decoration. ★☆☆☆☆

Meier tinplate covered lorry penny toy; unusual addition of an inertia drive increases value. ★★★☆☆

MEIER / METTOY

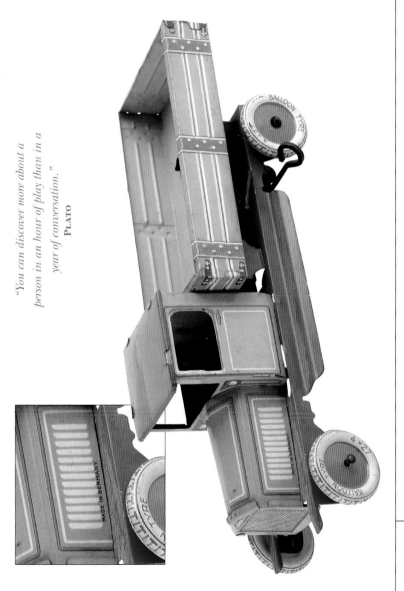

"You can discover more about a person in an hour of play than in a year of conversation." **PLATO**

Tinplate clockwork tipping lorry, in the style of Mettoy, with simple steering system; scarce model. ★★★ ☆☆☆

Mettoy tinplate racing car, with driver figure and clockwork mechanism. ★ ☆ ☆ ☆ ☆

Mettoy tinplate racing car, with clockwork mechanism and with original winding key and box. ★ ★ ☆ ☆ ☆

Mettoy "Sparking Racer," with push-and-go mechanism and sparking action, and with original box; scarce model. *1950s* ★ ☆ ☆ ☆

Schuco Studio toy car; has original box and paperwork, including salesman's instructions. *c.1935* ★☆☆☆☆

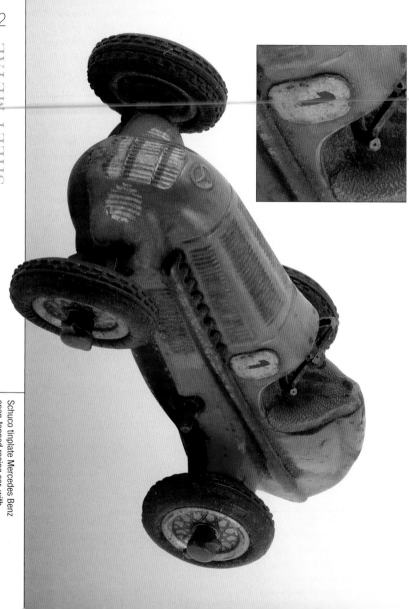

Schuco tinplate Mercedes Benz
open-topped racing car, with
clockwork mechanism. ★☆☆☆☆

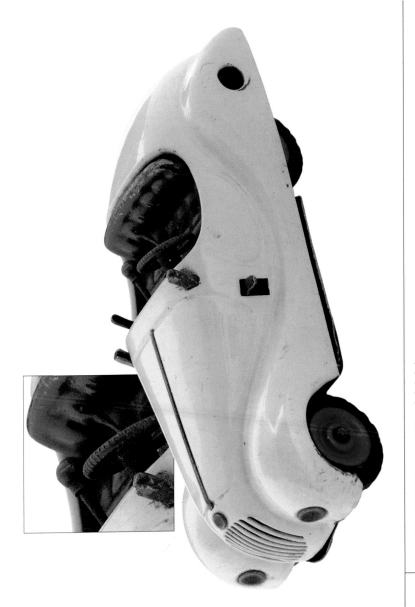

Prewar Schuco tinplate Examinco 4001. ★☆☆☆☆

"When I am grown to man's estate
I shall be very proud and great
And tell the other girls and boys
Not to meddle with my toys."
ROBERT LOUIS STEVENSON

Schuco Constructions 6065 breakdown
lorry, with working horn. ☆☆★★★

SCHUCO

The Schuco company produced high-quality toy cars from the mid-1930s onwards. Its founder, Heinrich Müller, personally designed the majority of his firm's products. The company, using modern production methods, produced large numbers of toys, shipping thousands of units a day from Müller's Nuremberg factory.

Schuco's classic toys were loosely based on luxury models such as BMWs and Porsches. Technical details such as working gears, handbrakes, and steering wheels added to their appeal. One ingenious model was the Command Car, issued in 1937, which could be made to start and stop by blowing air toward the roof. Another was the Turning Car, which would run up to a table-edge, swerve to avoid falling off, and keep going. Sales declined as the use of tin in the toy industry became obsolete in the 1960s, and the original Schuco factory went out of business in 1976.

Schuco streamlined 1010 Maybach "Turning Car," with clockwork mechanism. *1950* ★★☆☆

Schuco Constructions 6080 fire engine, with extending ladder. ★★★☆☆

British tinplate sedan car, with clockwork mechanism, orange finish, and printed decoration; the trunk with an operating lever.
★ ☆ ☆ ☆ ☆

Shackleton tinplate and diecast David Brown
Trackmaster 30 tractor, with clockwork mechanism;
rare model. ★★★☆☆

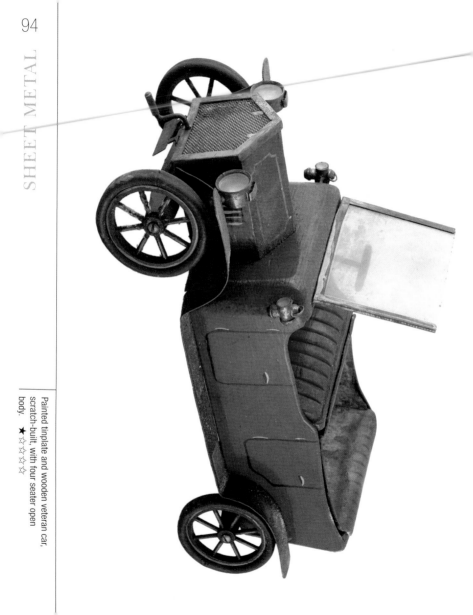

Painted tinplate and wooden veteran car, scratch-built, with four seater open body.
★ ☆☆☆☆

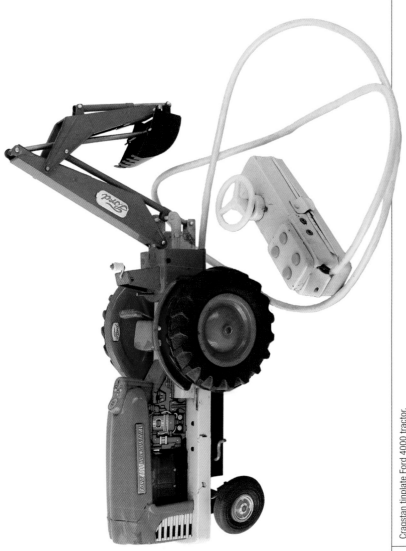

Cragstan tinplate Ford 4000 tractor,
with backhole and battery-operated remote
control unit. ★ ☆☆☆☆

TINPLATE BOATS

The earliest toy boats were probably the Noah's Ark toys carved from wood during the 18th century. When toymakers started to use tinplate in the mid-19th century they were able to offer children self-propelled model boats for the first time. German companies Märklin, Bing, Arnold, and Fleischmann produced a huge range of tin boats, some of which were powered by miniature steam engines that could run for an hour at a time. These steam-driven mechanisms were gradually superseded by clockwork, which was easier to run. Sutcliffe was the market leader in Britain, producing the first tinplate boat with a one-piece hull in 1932. Sutcliffe supplemented its wide range of boats with a number of submarines including the Nautilus and the Sea Wolf. Famous boats that made the news, such as the Bluebird water speed record breaking vessels, were reproduced by toymakers, allowing children to recreate dramatic scenes on the local pond.

FLEISCHMANN

Fleischmann tinplate ocean liner, with single funnel, cream and blue hull, brown decking and printed detail. With clockwork mechanism. ★★★☆☆

Sutcliffe tinplate Racer 1 speedboat, with "Racer 1" decal to stern. ★☆☆☆☆

Sutcliffe Nautilus submarine, with key. ★☆☆☆☆

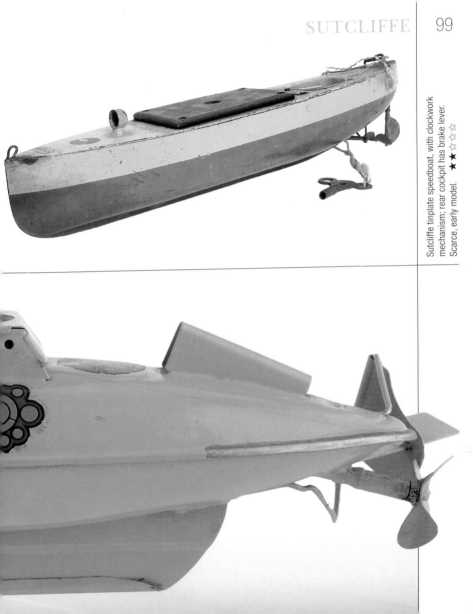

Sutcliffe tinplate speedboat, with clockwork mechanism; rear cockpit has brake lever. Scarce, early model. ★ ★ ☆ ☆ ☆

Tipp & Co. 1424 tinplate biplane, with metal propeller, removable wings, and number decals. ★☆☆☆☆

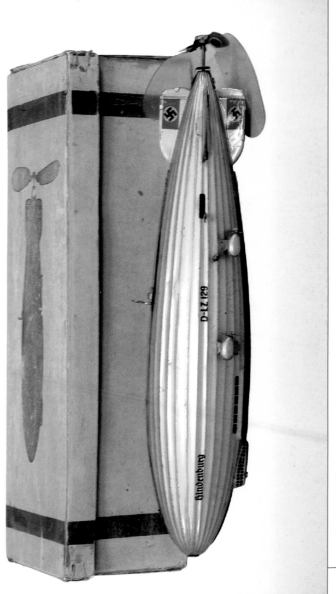

Tipp & Co. tinplate Hindenburg dirigible, with
celluloid propellers and swastika markings
on fins; with box. ★★★☆☆

DETAIL: Adjustable searchlight on back of truck.

3/6

FITTED
ADJUS
ELECT
SEARC

IC

HLIGHT LORRY

TRADE MARK

NES BROS. LTD. TRI-ANG WORKS LONDON S.W.19

TRI-ANG MINIC

Lines Bros., one of the biggest names in the British toy industry, launched the Tri-Ang brand in the 1940s. The early pressed steel cars were sold under the name "Minic," as was the successful range of toy ships. The original Minic range included plant vehicles such as dust carts and breakdown trucks, many of which had working clockwork components. From the 1960s, Tri-Ang marketed a range of cars and accessories called "Minic Motorways," which were intended to work alongside Tri-Ang's model railway sets. Minic products were sold all over the world, and stock varied from country to country. Prices for pressed steel Minic toys dating from the 1940s and 50s can be high, particularly if they are complete with all their original packaging.

Tri-Ang Minic searchlight truck, with clockwork mechanism and gas can, and with original box; scarce model. ★★☆☆☆

Tri-Ang Minic 21M second series tinplate transport van, with gas can and original box; early model. ★★☆☆☆

Tri-Ang Minic 32M second series tinplate dustcart, with clockwork mechanism, and with gas can and box; early model. ★ ★ ☆ ☆ ☆

SHEET METAL

Tri-Ang Minic 85M transport van, with clockwork mechanism; has original box. ★ ☆☆☆☆

Tri-Ang Minic 86M tipper truck, with red plastic hubs and black tires; has original box. ★ ☆ ☆

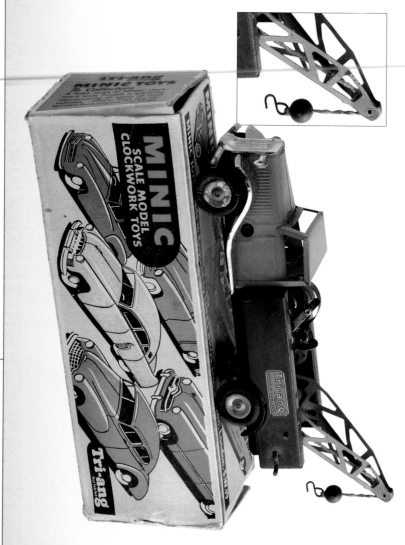

Tri-Ang Minic 48M tinplate breakdown truck, with diecast hubs; has original box and instruction sheet. ★★☆☆☆

Tri-Ang Minic 8M second series open tourer, with clockwork mechanism, and with original box; early model. ★ ☆☆☆☆

Tri-Ang Minic 39M second series taxi cab, with gas can and original box. ★★☆☆☆

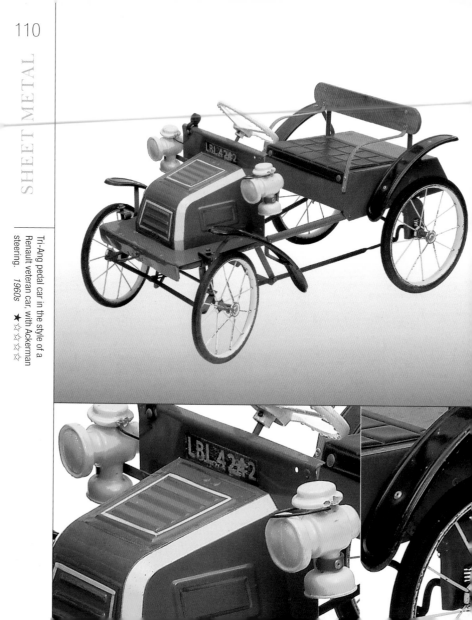

Tri-Ang pedal car in the style of a Renault veteran car, with Ackerman steering. *1960s* ★☆☆☆☆

Tri-Ang Frog Mk IV interceptor fighter aircraft, in Belgian flying colors, with original orange box. ★ ☆☆☆☆

Tri-Ang Minic gas tanker, with clockwork mechanism, and with original box; rare model. *c.1940* ★★☆☆☆

Tri-Ang Minic 1M CF Ford Army saloon, with clockwork mechanism, and with original box. *c.1945* ★★☆☆☆

"As men get older, the toys get more expensive."

MARVIN DAVIS, BILLIONAIRE

Tri-Ang Minic tinplate delivery van, with clockwork mechanism and key. ★ ☆☆☆☆

MINIC TRANSPORT

ROAD, RAIL AIR & SEA

EXPRESS SERVICE

TRI-ANG
Made in England

DETAIL: Label on side of truck.

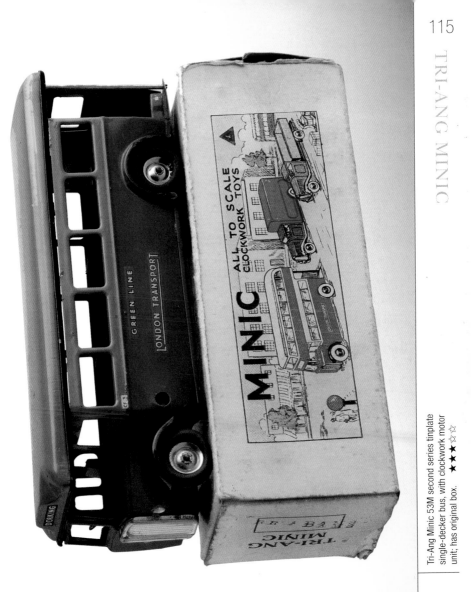

Tri-Ang Minic 53M second series tinplate single-decker bus, with clockwork motor unit; has original box. ★★★☆☆

Tri-Ang Minic 60M double-decker bus, with diecast wheels and London Transport logo; has original box. ★★★☆☆

Tri-Ang Minic second series Nuffield tractor, with clockwork mechanism; has original box. ★ ☆☆☆☆

p.32

p.67

p.405

p.53

p.116

p.222

p.406

p.27

p.172

p.163

p.230

p.115

p.310

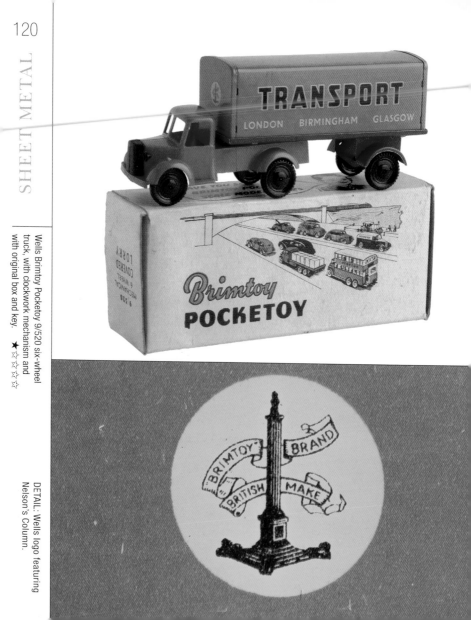

Wells Brimtoy Pocketoy 9/520 six-wheel truck, with clockwork mechanism and with original box and key. ★ ☆☆☆☆

DETAIL: Wells logo featuring Nelson's Column.

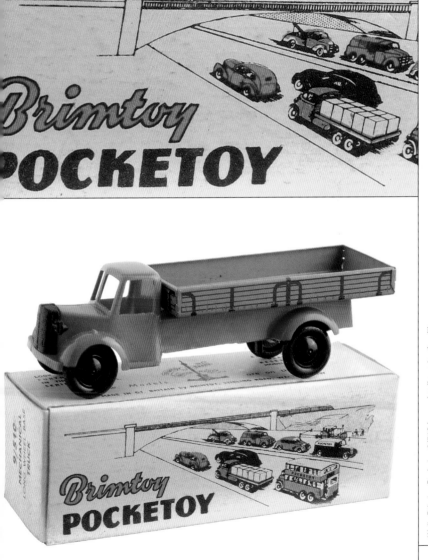

Wells Brimtoy Pocketoy 9/510 long-wheelbase truck, with tinplate body, red plastic cab and chassis, and clockwork mechanism; has original box and key. ★ ☆☆☆

MMN tinplate fire truck, with water canister and fireman figures. ★★★★★

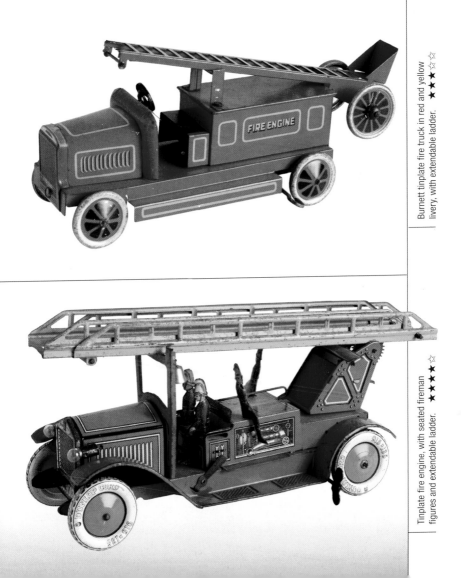

Burnett tinplate fire truck in red and yellow livery, with extendable ladder. ★ ★ ★ ☆ ☆

Tinplate fire engine, with seated fireman figures and extendable ladder. ★ ★ ★ ★ ☆

Dayton pressed steel Hillclimber fire engine, with driver figure, ladders, and wheel. ★★★☆☆

Structro tinplate tractor, with clockwork mechanism and original winding crank. *1920s* ★ ★ ☆ ☆ ☆

Andre Citroën tinplate open tourer, with silvered running boards, leatherette seats, and gearstick linked to clockwork motor. ★★★★☆

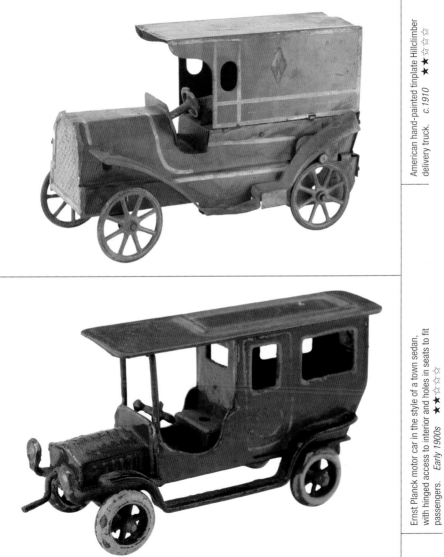

American hand-painted tinplate Hillclimber delivery truck. *c.1910* ★★ ☆☆☆

Ernst Planck motor car in the style of a town sedan, with hinged access to interior and holes in seats to fit passengers. *Early 1900s* ★★ ☆☆☆

This fire vehicle has printed details including a radiator, fireman figures, and a coat of arms.

French tinplate fire vehicle, with tinplate tires marked "Dunlop" and clockwork mechanism; early model. ★★☆☆☆

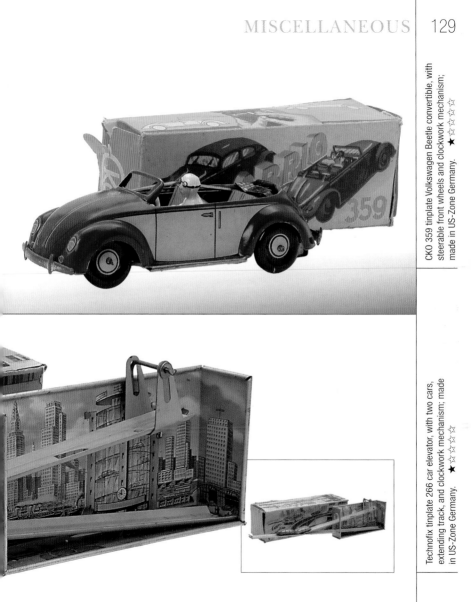

CKO 359 tinplate Volkswagen Beetle convertible, with steerable front wheels and clockwork mechanism; made in US-Zone Germany. ★ ☆ ☆ ☆

Technofix tinplate 266 car elevator, with two cars, extending track, and clockwork mechanism; made in US-Zone Germany. ★ ☆ ☆ ☆

Tinplate "United States" cruise liner, with fine
detailing and original box. ★★★☆☆

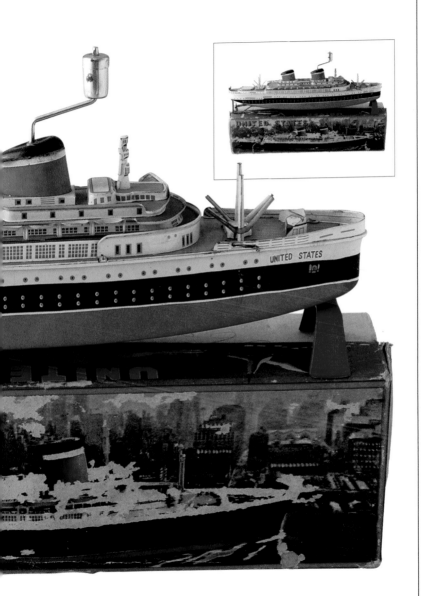

SHEET METAL

Rossignol tinplate Renault gas tanker, with simple
steering system, printed decoration, and clockwork
mechanism; rare model.   ★★★
                                    ★★☆☆

ESSENCE POUR AUTO MOBILES

SHELL

C.R
MADE IN FRANCE

ESSENCE POUR AUTO MOBILES

SHELL

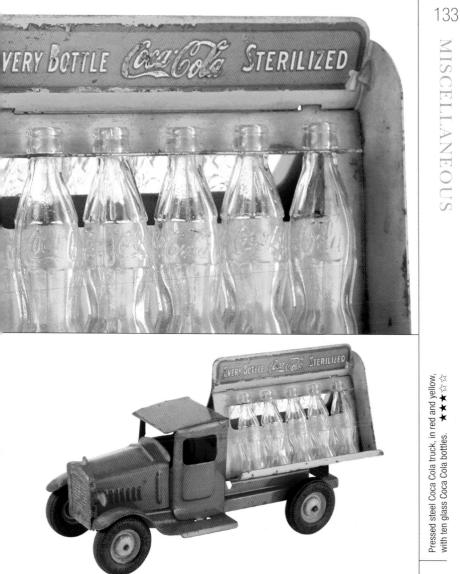

Pressed steel Coca Cola truck, in red and yellow,
with ten glass Coca Cola bottles.

★★☆☆
★★★

Tinplate and plastic Boeing 727 aircraft, with battery-operated mechanism. ★ ☆ ☆ ☆ ☆

Joustra tinplate Super G Constellation aircraft in Air France livery, with battery-powered mechanism; scarce model. ★ ★ ☆ ☆ ☆

Tinplate twin-engined transport aircraft, with
red details and propellers'. ★ ☆☆☆☆

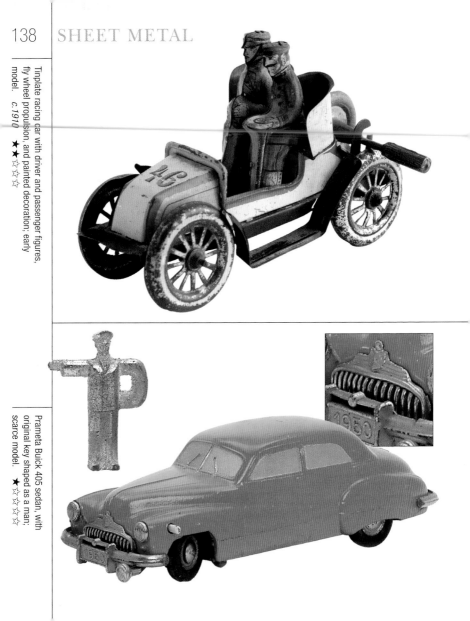

Tinplate racing car with driver and passenger figures, fly wheel propulsion, and painted decoration; early model. *c.1910* ★★☆☆☆

Prameta Buick 405 sedan, with original key shaped as a man; scarce model. ★☆☆☆☆

This truck is in the style of a Magirus Deutz truck, and is probably German.

Tinplate military truck with opening driver's door and hinged shell box, towing field gun with diecast barrel. ★ ☆☆☆☆

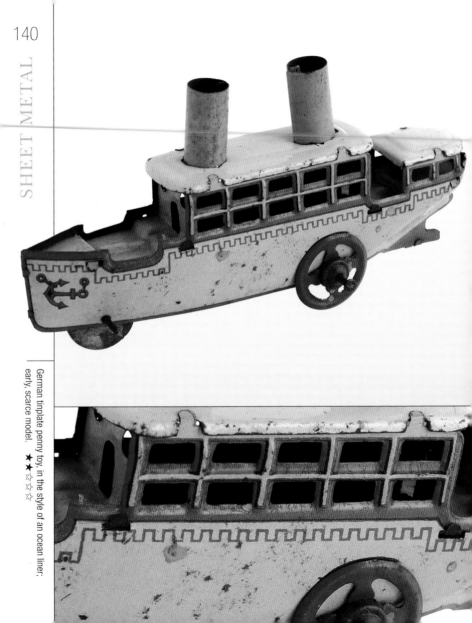

German tinplate penny toy, in the style of an ocean liner; early, scarce model. ★★☆☆☆

Features include a conning tower, bow platform, and moveable dive planes.

Tinplate submarine, with small operating cannon, rudder, and clockwork four-blade propeller; has original key. ★★★☆☆

CAST IRON

The construction of toys from cast iron was almost exclusively an American phenomenon. Iron foundries in the industrial northeast, originally built to provide parts for agricultural and military hardware, were used increasingly in the manufacture of consumer goods toward the end of the 19th century. Entrepreneurial minds soon realized that the popularity of imported metal toys from Germany represented an opportunity for American industry and seized it. Most cast iron toys were created from molds cast from miniature brass replicas of real cars. After casting, the component iron pieces were riveted together, finished and painted. This process made toys that were extremely durable, and the care put into decorating them has ensured that they remain collectible today. During the WWII, iron was unavailable for peacetime luxuries such as toys, and most of the foundries never resumed production.

DETAIL: Original driver and rubber-stamped lettering.

ARCADE

Arcade Manufacturing started life in 1855 as a cast iron foundry in Chicago. The firm diversified into toys in 1908, issuing a cast iron model taxi cab in 1921. The taxi was based on Chicago's distinctive Yellow Cab Co. fleet, founded by John Hertz in 1915 and still one of the largest cab firms in the US. It was an immediate success, particularly among city children. In order to appeal to the rural market, Arcade released a model Fordson tractor the next year, and followed this with a range of farm machinery reputedly sturdy enough to be used in the garden.

Arcade toy cars and farm vehicles are easy to identify as most carry the company logo. The famous Arcade taxi cabs were made in a variety of colors and designs – very often, like the Yellow Cabs, as promotional issues for real taxi companies.

Arcade Yellow Cab: the company's first promotional toy.　1921　★★★☆☆

Arcade Ford four-door sedan, with spoked nickel wheels, Model T features, and "Bozum Motor Co. Mitchell SD" advertising on roof. ★★☆☆☆

Arcade fire chief's car, with gold-trimmed cast bell on hood and "Chief" embossed on the doors. c.1932 ★★★ ☆☆

Arcade Pontiac taxi cab, with nickel grille and lights, rubber tires, and remains of label on rear. c.1935 ★★★ ☆☆

Arcade cast iron racer, with two cast figures; rare model. *1936* ★★★★★

Arcade cast iron racer, in silver, with racing number "8," white rubber tires, and driver figure. *1933* ★☆☆☆☆

I often think that could we creep behind the actor's eyes, we would find an attic of forgotten toys and a copy of the Domesday Book.

LAURENCE OLIVIER

Arcade cast iron contractor's dump wagon in blue, with spoked nickel wheels. Rare, early model. *1920s* ★★☆☆☆

Arcade cast iron Mack ladder truck, with spoked wheels and extendable ladder. ★★★☆☆

Arcade cast iron Fordson tractor, with embossed wheels, nickel driver figure, and rubber tires. *1920s* ★★☆☆☆

Arcade cast iron Oliver plow, with silver blades, spoked nickel wheels, and side gear. *1920s–30s* ★ ★ ☆ ☆ ☆

ON THE FARM

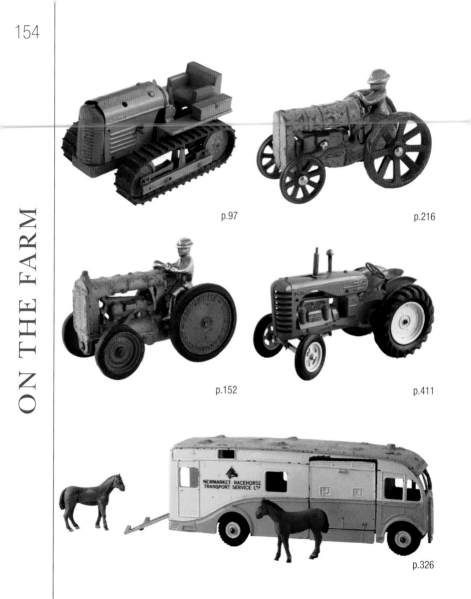

p.97

p.216

p.152

p.411

NEWMARKET RACEHORSE
TRANSPORT SERVICE LTD

p.326

p.334

p.190

p.162

p.158

p.159

Arcade cast iron McCormick Deering open-bed spreader, with three rotating nickel shafts. ★★☆☆☆

Arcade cast iron Ford 9N tractor, with driver figure and black wooden wheels; rare salesman's sample. *1941* ★★☆☆☆

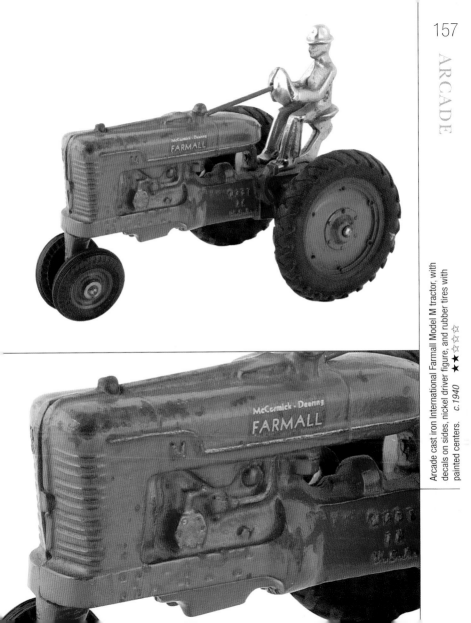

Arcade cast iron International Farmall Model M tractor, with decals on sides, nickel driver figure, and rubber tires with painted centers. *c.1940* ★★☆☆☆

Arcade cast iron Allis-Chalmers WC tractor, with "Allis-Chalmers" decal, nickel driver and drawbar, and black rubber tires. 1940–41 ★★☆☆☆

Arcade cast iron John Deere A tractor, with rubber tires and nickel driver figure. *c.1940* ★★★☆☆

Arcade cast iron Oliver Superior spreader, with three rotating nickel shafts, rubber tires, and decals on sides. *1940–41* ★★★☆☆

Arcade cast iron Avery tractor in black, with spoked red wheels. *Mid-1920s* ★☆☆☆☆

Arcade cast iron Avery tractor in green, with spoked red wheels. This model was also available in gray. *1926–28* ★★☆☆☆

Arcade cast iron double-decker bus, with nickel grille, rubber tires, cast driver figure, and three passenger figures. *c.1940* ★★☆☆

DETAIL: Amos and Andy, with dog.

DENT

Henry Dent and four other partners founded the Dent Hardware Company in Fullerton, Pennsylvania, in 1895. Like many other firms making cast iron toys, Dent Hardware originally made components for consumer goods but quickly became better known for making toys.

Dent's first model horse-drawn vehicles were followed by cars, buses, tractors, and road construction vehicles such as graders and steam shovels. One of the most striking models was Dent's bright orange "Fresh Air Taxi," based on the popular cartoon strip "Amos 'n' Andy." Today, the most valuable Dent models are the early chauffeur-driven touring cars with their elegant passengers. By the late 1930s, however, competition from firms that used cheaper diecasting technology meant the end of the line for Dent toys.

Dent cast iron "Fresh Air Taxi," ridden by Amos and Andy from the popular radio show "Amos 'n' Andy." ★★★★ ★★★☆

"As dry leaves that before the wild hurricane fly,
when they meet with an obstacle, mount to the sky,
so up to the house-top the coursers they flew,
with the sleigh full of toys, and St. Nicholas too."

CLEMENT CLARKE MOORE

Dent cast iron express wagon, with horse and driver
and removable bench seat. ★ ☆☆☆☆

Dent cast iron road grader, with driver figure holding two wheel controls; rare model. ★ ☆☆☆☆

Dent cast iron express truck in red, with driver figure and yellow spoked wheels. *1920s* ★★☆☆☆

Dent cast iron coupé, with yellow disk wheels. Cast driver's head is visible through window. ★ ☆ ☆ ☆ ☆

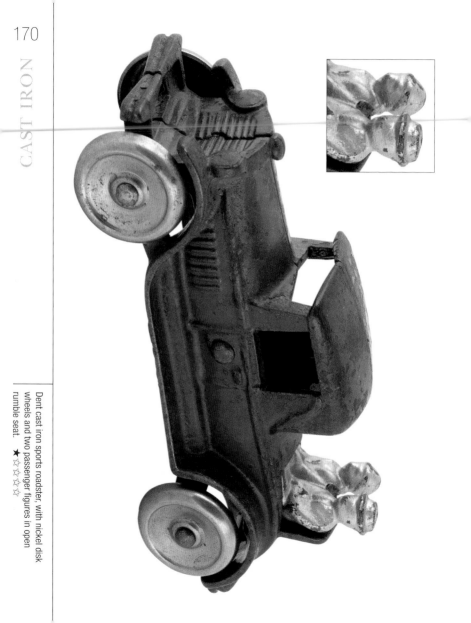

Dent cast iron sports roadster, with nickel disk wheels and two passenger figures in open rumble seat. ★☆☆☆☆

Dent cast iron fire chief's coupé, with cast bell on hood, embossed door, cast driver figure, and nickel disk wheels. ★ ★ ★ ☆ ☆

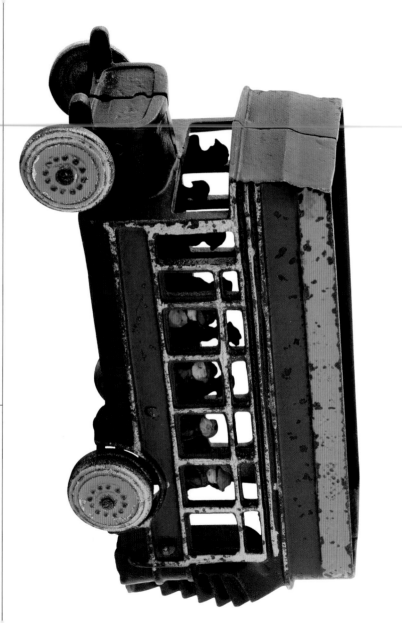

Freidag cast iron double-decker bus, with cast metal wheels and passenger and driver figures. ★★★☆☆

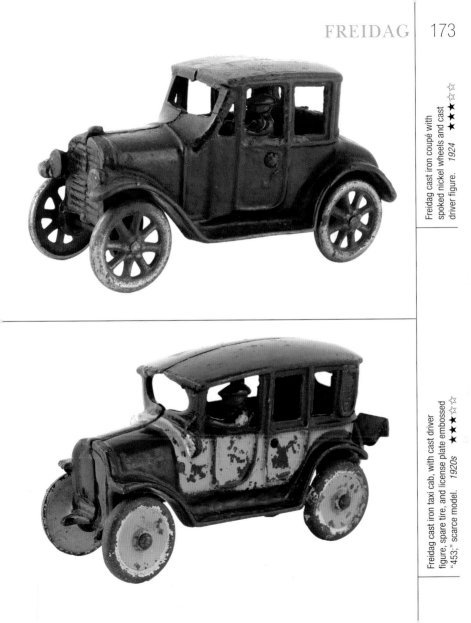

Freidag cast iron coupé with spoked nickel wheels and cast driver figure.   *1924*   ★ ★ ★ ☆ ☆

Freidag cast iron taxi cab, with cast driver figure, spare tire, and license plate embossed "453;" scarce model.   *1920s*   ★ ★ ★ ☆ ☆

DETAIL: Hubley logo decal.

HUBLEY

Originally founded to manufacture model trains, Hubley came to dominate the market for cast iron toy cars in the US after a management shake-up in 1909. Hubley capitalized on the popularity of the "five and dime" stores that offered cheap goods to the public, realizing that they were an ideal outlet for affordable quality toys. As more Americans came to own cars, more American children wanted toy cars, which Hubley were in the perfect position to offer. In addition, Hubley produced a range of cast iron aircraft called "Lindy Gliders" after Charles Lindbergh, the famous aviator; this kind of shrewd marketing was another reason for Hubley's success. They also secured the rights to produce toys based on Harley Davidson motorcycles and Bell Telephone trucks.

Hubley cast iron 665 coupé; available in five different sizes, the largest being the most sought-after. ★★★☆☆

Hubley Golden Arrow racer, with eight cylinders on hood. The twelve-cylinder version is more valuable. *1931–41* ★ ☆☆☆☆

Hubley cast iron Kiddie Toy racer, with driver figure and rubber tires. ★ ☆☆☆☆

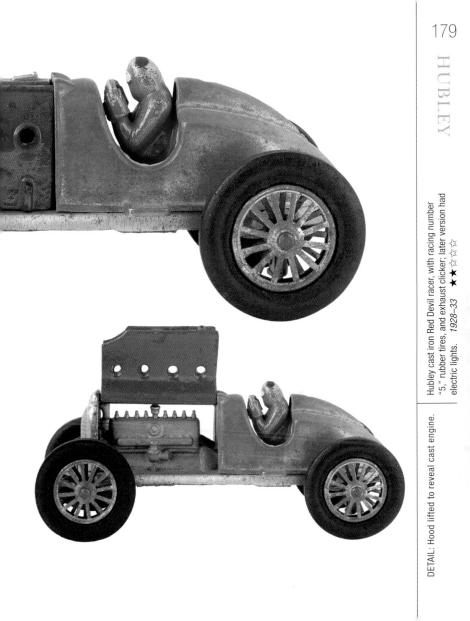

Hubley cast iron Red Devil racer, with racing number "5," rubber tires, and exhaust clicker; later version had electric lights. *1928–33* ★ ☆ ☆ ☆

DETAIL: Hood lifted to reveal cast engine.

Hubley cast iron flame exhaust racer; the turning wheels activate a mechanism that moves red "flames" up and down. ★★★★☆

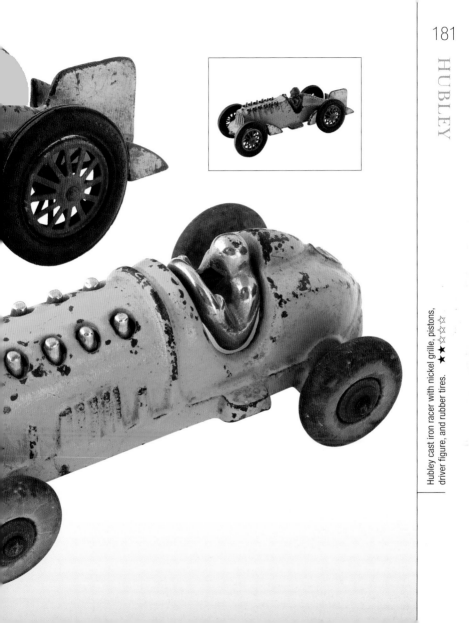

Hubley cast iron racer with nickel grille, pistons, driver figure, and rubber tires.
★ ★ ☆ ☆ ☆

Hubley cast iron racer, with embossed racing number "7" on hood, seated driver figure, and white rubber tires with red wooden hubs. ★☆☆☆☆

Hubley cast iron open racer, with twin seats and yellow spoked wheels; rare model. ★ ☆ ☆ ☆

Hubley cast iron racer in red with gold-trimmed hood, and with driver figure and tank to rear; early model. ★ ★ ★ ☆ ☆

Hubley cast iron coupé, with driver figure, disk wheels painted red and silver, and spare mounted on trunk. ★★★☆☆

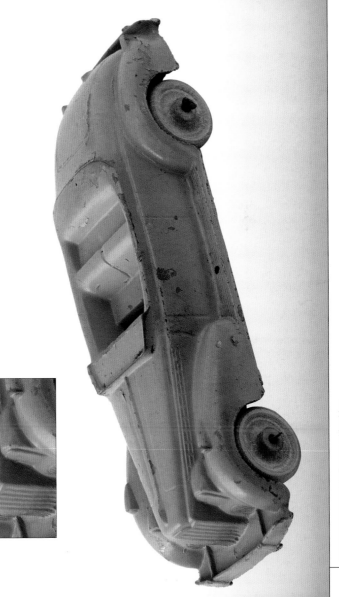

Hubley cast iron Kiddie Toy car, with rubber wheels. ★ ☆☆☆☆

Hubley cast iron ladder truck, with cast driver figure, rubber tires, and original tin ladders. ★ ☆☆☆☆

Hubley cast iron fire pump truck, with cast wheels and integral driver.
★ ☆☆☆☆

Hubley cast iron Monarch bulldozer, with black traction treads; interior cam mechanism produces articulated motion when bulldozer is pushed. c. 1932 ★★☆☆☆

HUBLEY

Hubley cast iron General shovel truck, with rubber wheels and nickel-plated shovel boom. ★★★☆☆

Hubley cast iron Oliver "Orchard" tractor, with separately cast driver and seat frame and embossed wheel arches; in excellent condition. *c.1940* ★ ★ ★ ☆ ☆

HUBLEY

Hubley cast iron horse-drawn fire truck, with cast wheels, two fireman figures, and ladder. *1920s* ★ ☆ ☆ ☆

Hubley cast iron Lindy Glider pull-along aircraft, in gray, with "Hubley" transfer on tail. *1928–33* ★★☆☆☆

Hubley cast iron Lindy Glider pull-along aircraft, with pilot figure.   *1930s*   ★ ★ ☆ ☆ ☆

KENTON

Based in Kenton, Ohio, the Kenton Hardware Company was founded in the 1890s. The earliest vehicles produced included farm drays and a variety of horse-drawn carts and carriages. However, it was not until Lewis Bixler – with years of experience in the toy trade – joined the firm in 1909 that Kenton took off.

Kenton's managers were instrumental in founding Toy Manufacturers of the USA, a trade organization that still survives today. The firm's output was extraordinary; some sources estimate that 5,000 distinct models were produced by Kenton during the 50 or so years that it made toys. A huge range of construction vehicles and trucks, many of which had moving parts, showed Kenton's commitment to realism and education, and has ensured that devoted fans will collect Kenton model vehicles for many years to come.

Kenton cast iron horse-drawn two-seat Surrey carriage, with driver and passenger figures. *c.1918* ★ ★ ☆ ☆ ☆

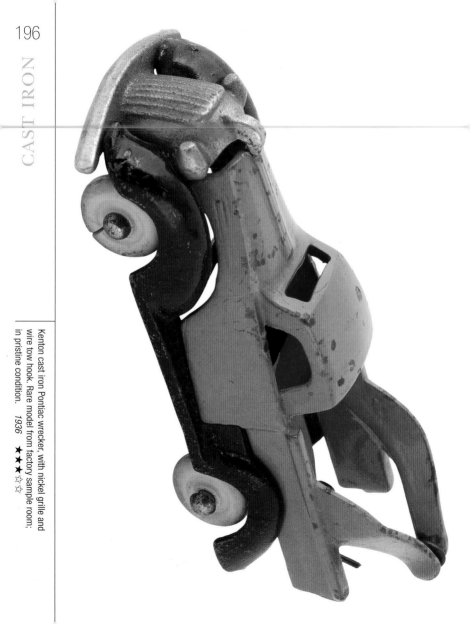

Kenton cast iron Pontiac wrecker, with nickel grille and wire tow hook. Rare model from factory sample room; in pristine condition. *1936* ★★★☆☆

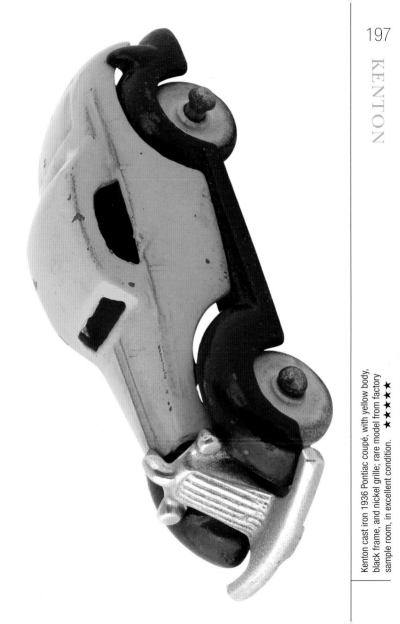

Kenton cast iron 1936 Pontiac coupé, with yellow body, black frame, and nickel grille; rare model from factory sample room, in excellent condition. ★★★★★

Kenton cast iron Pontiac sedan, with red body, black frame, nickel grille, and white rubber tires. From factory sample room; never used. ★★★☆☆

Kenton cast iron Phaeton, with blue painted body, silver frame, nickel grille, and white rubber tires. ★★★☆

Kenton cast iron Pontiac fire engine, with nickel boiler cover and cast driver; one of only two known examples with this type of grille. *1936* ★★★☆☆

Kenton cast iron fire chief's coupé, with cast bell on hood, embossed doors, cast driver figure, and nickel disk wheels. ★ ★ ★ ☆ ☆

Kenton cast iron National wagon, with embossed sides, pull handle, and rubber tires. ★ ☆ ☆ ☆

Kenton cast iron Peerless racer, painted silver, with "Peerless" embossed on hood, disk wheels, and original driver. *Early 1900s* ★★☆☆☆

Kenton cast iron open roadster, with seated driver and painted disk wheels. *1920s* ★☆☆☆☆

Kenton cast iron sedan, with disk wheels and separately cast driver; in excellent condition. *c.1925* ★★★☆☆

Kenton cast iron auto dray, with spoked wheels, embossed letters on sides, and original driver figure; early model. ★★★☆☆

VINTAGE VEHICLES

p.217

p.166

p.67

p.195

p.26

p.149

p.20   p.24   p.38

p.272   p.21   p.298

p.17   p.111

VINTAGE VEHICLES

Kilgore cast iron Sea Gull aircraft, with nickel-plated wheels and wing-mounted engine.

★★★☆☆

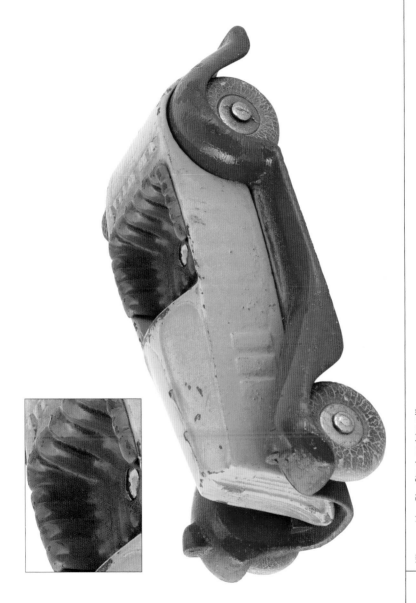

Kilgore cast iron Blue Streak roadster, with separately cast embossed seat and nickel hubs. *c.1930*   ★ ★ ★ ☆ ☆

Kilgore cast iron Model T Ford coupé, with spoked
nickel wheels.   *c.1927*   ★★★★☆

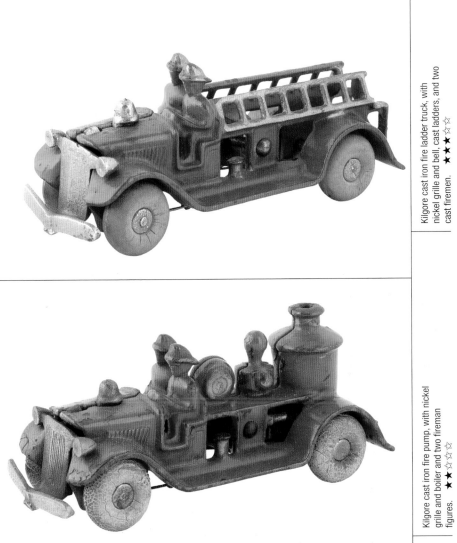

Kilgore cast iron fire ladder truck, with nickel grille and bell, cast ladders, and two cast firemen. ★ ★ ☆ ☆

Kilgore cast iron fire pump, with nickel grille and boiler and two fireman figures. ★ ☆ ☆ ☆

Williams cast iron 1936 Ford coupé, with nickel grille. This model was one of a set of four deluxe toy cars. ★★★☆☆

Williams cast iron racer, with cast side pipes painted in red, driver figure, and rubber tires.   *c.1936*   ★ ★ ★ ☆ ☆

Williams cast iron Model T Ford coupé, with silver-painted, spoked wheels.   ★ ☆ ☆ ☆ ☆

Williams cast iron gas tanker, with "Gasoline Motor Oil Fruehauf Co." embossed on sides, and with spoked nickel wheels. *1920s* ★★☆☆☆

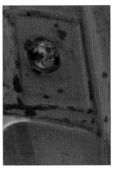

Williams cast iron dump truck, in red with green trailer, and with metal hubs and rubber wheels. ★★☆☆☆

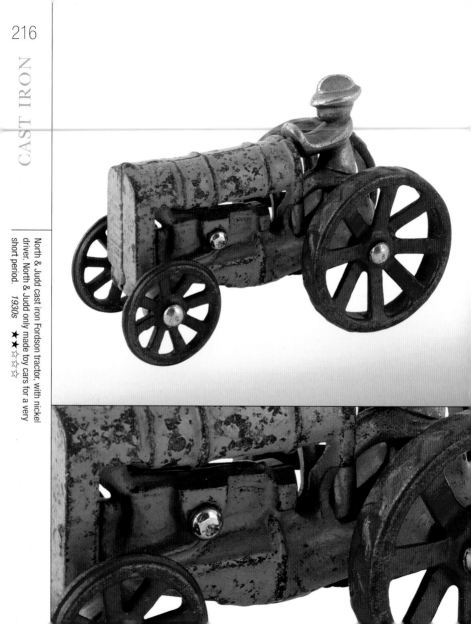

North & Judd cast iron Fordson tractor, with nickel driver. North & Judd only made toy cars for a very short period. *1930s* ★★☆☆☆

Harris cast iron "Mama Katzenjammer" open cart; kicking mule is cast with legs attached to cart. ★ ★ ★ ☆ ☆

Shimer cast iron Conestoga "Eldorado" ox-drawn wagon, with embossed sides and driver figure; rare model. ★ ★ ☆ ☆ ☆

Champion cast iron racer, with green
hood, red body, and blue driver, embossed
"Champion" behind seat. ★ ★ ★ ☆ ☆

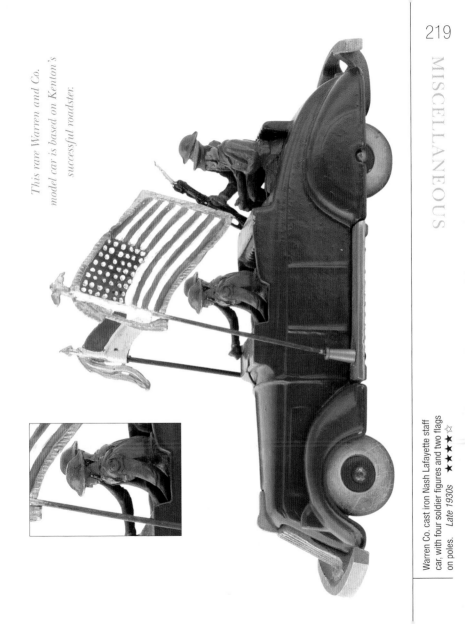

This rare Warren and Co. model car is based on Kenton's successful roadster.

Warren Co. cast iron Nash Lafayette staff car, with four soldier figures and two flags on poles.   *Late 1930s*   ★★★☆

CORGI

Mettoy launched its Corgi brand in 1956, having expanded into diecast toys from the munitions work it had done during the war. This first range comprised classic British saloon cars such as the Austin Cambridge and Riley Pathfinder. Over the years, Corgi toys developed a reputation for innovation. To distinguish Corgi cars from those of arch rival Dinky, the company introduced plastic windows to its models and, in 1959, Corgi was the first toy manufacturer to use real spring suspension.

Accolades awarded to Corgi include two Queen's Awards for Industry and the 1965 UK Toy of the Year Award for the James Bond Aston Martin DB5. The company has also weathered its share of storms, including a warehouse fire in 1969. Corgi continues to release limited edition models today.

Corgi London Transport Routemaster double-decker bus, with original box and paper slip. ★☆☆☆☆

Corgi 339 Mini Cooper S, with original box; this model is a replica of the 1967 Monte Carlo winner. ★☆☆☆☆

Corgi 225 Austin 7 Mini saloon, with original box; variation on the standard model, which has red seats. ★☆☆☆☆

Corgi 450 Austin Mini van in metallic mid-green with red interiors, and with original box. ★☆☆☆☆

Corgi 226 Morris Mini Minor: model of the first iconic "Mini," manufactured between 1959–62. ★☆☆☆☆

Corgi 277 Monkeemobile, from "The Monkees" television series, with "Monkees" logo. ★ ☆☆☆☆

"Taking a child to the toy store is the nearest thing to a death wish parents can have."

FRED G. GOSMAN

Corgi 150S Vanwall Formula 1 Grand Prix
car, racing number "25," with original
box.   1961–65   ★ ☆☆☆☆

Corgi 1101 Carrimore car transporter, with original box. ★☆☆☆☆

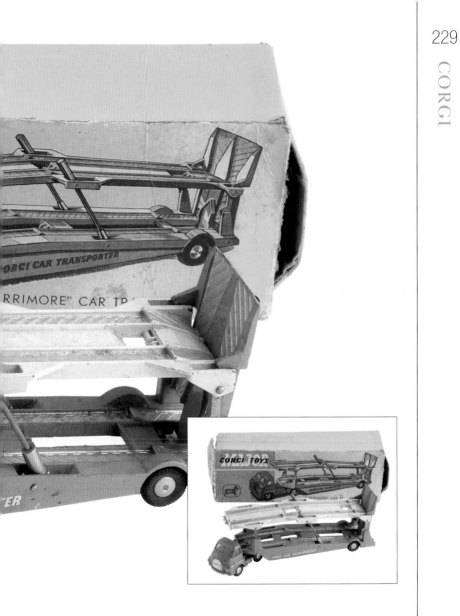

Corgi 1110 Bedford S-type articulated tanker, with "Mobilgas" logos on sides and rear, and with original box. ★ ☆☆☆☆

Corgi Major Toys 1120 Midland motorway express coach, with original box. ★ ☆☆☆☆

Corgi 17 gift set, comprising Land Rover and trailer with Ferrari racing car; has original box and insert. ★★☆☆☆

Corgi 2 gift set, comprising Land Rover, Rice horse trailer, and pony, with original box. ★☆☆☆☆

Corgi 19 gift set of circus vehicles, in original box with inner display sleeve and packing. ★★☆☆☆

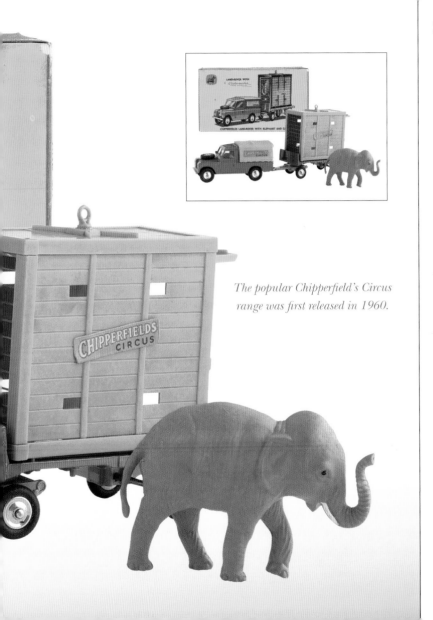

The popular Chipperfield's Circus range was first released in 1960.

CHIPPERFIELDS
CIRCUS

Corgi 426 Chipperfield's Circus mobile booking office, with original box. ★ ★ ★ ☆ ☆

Corgi 1121 Major crane truck, in Chipperfield's Circus livery, with original box. ★ ☆☆☆☆

Corgi 245 Buick Riviera in gold, with original box. ★ ☆ ☆ ☆ ☆

Corgi 325 Ford Mustang Fastback 2+2 competition model, with original box. ★ ☆☆☆☆

Corgi 240 Fiat Ghia 600 Jolly, with original box and packing. ★★ ☆☆☆

Corgi 16 gift set, comprising "Ecurie Ecosse" racing car transporter with 150S Vanwall, 151A Mk II Lotus, and 152S BRM; has original box. ★★★☆☆

AND THREE RACING CARS

DETAIL: Top of transporter, with cars in place.

MERCHANDISE

Perhaps more than any other toy manufacturer, Corgi has become associated with cool cars from cult television series and blockbusting films. The most famous examples are James Bond's Aston Martin DB5 and the Batmobile, but Corgi has issued dozens of other model vehicles based on popular motorized icons.

The shows best suited to be immortalized in this way were the ones in which the real star was the car. General Lee (the Dodge Charger featured in "The Dukes of Hazzard") and KITT (Michael Knight's Pontiac Trans Am in "Knight Rider") are all-time favorites. Quirkier vehicles, such as the Yellow Submarine from the Beatles' film of the same name, Chitty Chitty Bang Bang, and the Monkeemobile, have also made the transition from screen to toy store thanks to Corgi.

Corgi 803 Yellow Submarine, from Beatles animated film of the same name, with original box; scarce variation with red hatches. 1970–71 ★★★ ★★ ☆☆

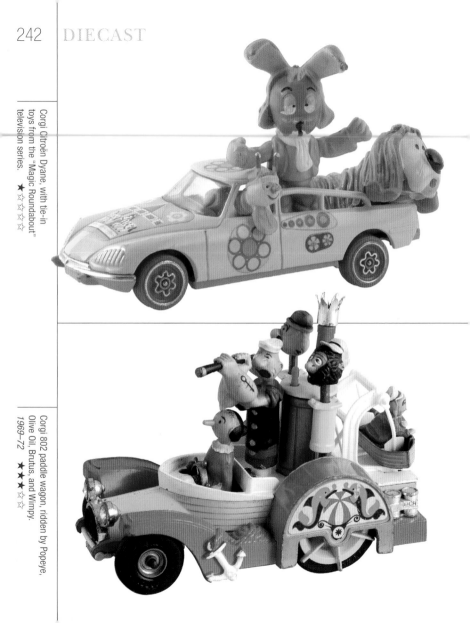

Corgi Citroën Dyane, with tie-in toys from the "Magic Roundabout" television series. ★☆☆☆☆

Corgi 802 paddle wagon, ridden by Popeye, Olive Oil, Brutus, and Wimpy. 1969–72 ★★★☆☆

Corgi model of "Chitty Chitty Bang Bang,"
released in 1968, the same year as
the film. ★ ☆ ☆ ☆ ☆

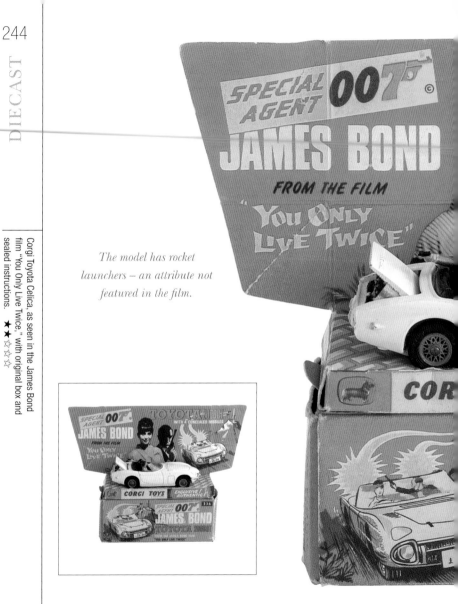

The model has rocket launchers – an attribute not featured in the film.

Corgi Toyota Celica, as seen in the James Bond film "You Only Live Twice," with original box and sealed instructions. ★★☆☆☆

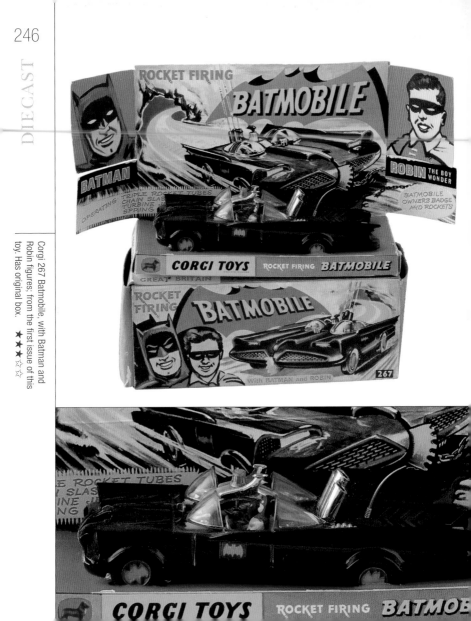

Corgi 267 Batmobile, with Batman and
Robin figures: from the first issue of this
toy. Has original box. ★★★☆☆

Corgi 256 Volkswagen 1200, with African safari trim and model rhinoceros: has original box. *1965–68* ★ ★ ☆ ☆ ☆

FILM & FANTASY

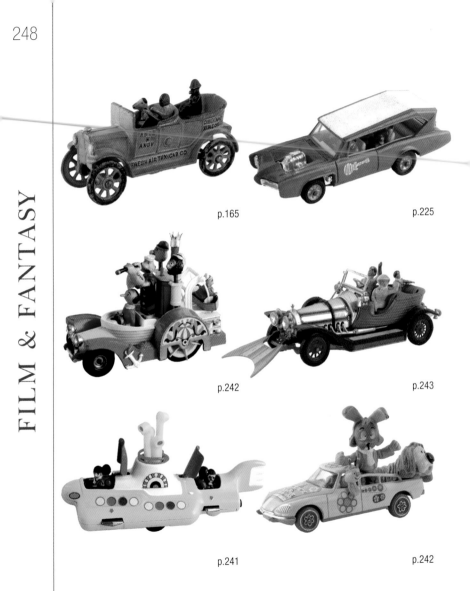

p.165

p.225

p.242

p.243

p.241

p.242

p.251

p.244

p.246

p.268

THE JAMES BOND COLLECTION
"Goldfinger's" Rolls Royce SET

This set represents Rolls Royce Phantom III from the movie " Goldfinger ". The set contained the figures of Goldfinger and Odd'Job. This edition is strictly limited at 100 sets only.

Certificat N°. 027/100

Rolls Royce Phantom III 1939

Goldfinger's

p.417

FILM & FANTASY

Corgi prototype 36 Tarzan gift set, with diorama background and illustrated box. ★★☆☆☆

How to make your
3-D Jungle Panorama

Comment réaliser
Diorama 3-D de la Jungle

So wird das 3-D
Dschungel-Panorama gebaut

Tree House
Cabane
Baumhaus

2 Tarzan figures are provided for different play situations.

2 figurines de Tarzan sont inclues pour réaliser des scènes différentes.

Enthält 2 Tarzanfiguren fuer verschiedene Spielsituationen.

Vines
Lianes
Schlingpflanzen

*The set comprises a green and white
zebra-striped Land Rover, trailer with
opening roof hatch, dinghy, and cast
human and animal figures.*

GIFT SET 36

GIFT SET 36

Tarzan · CORGI GIFT SET 36

Corgi 1106 Decca mobile airfield radar van, in cream and orange striped livery, with original box. ★ ☆☆☆☆

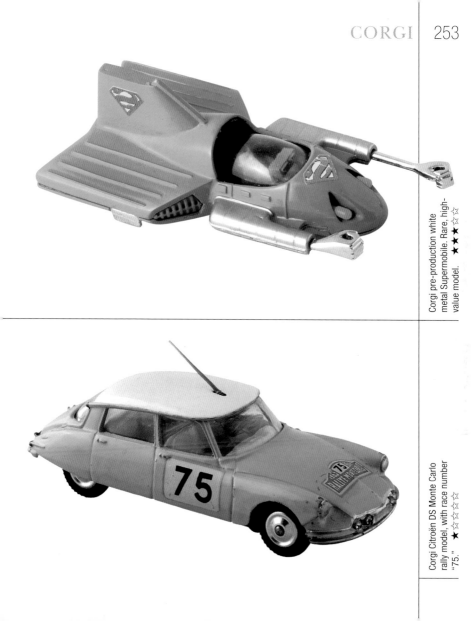

Corgi pre-production white metal Supermobile. Rare, high-value model. ★ ★ ★ ☆ ☆

Corgi Citroën DS Monte Carlo rally model, with race number "75." ★ ☆ ☆ ☆ ☆

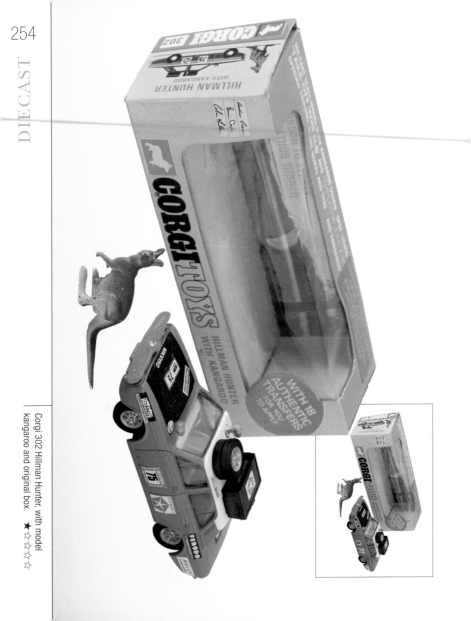

Corgi 302 Hillman Hunter, with model kangaroo and original box. ★☆☆☆☆

*Corgi's range of Chipperfield's Circus
toys came with a variety of animals
including lions, rhinos, tigers,
and polar bears.*

Corgi "Chipperfield's Performing Poodles" gift set, with car based
on Chevrolet Impala; has original box. ★ ☆ ☆ ☆ ☆

Corgi Citroën DS "Le Dandy Coupé" in burgundy, with opening doors and boot. Original car was created by Citroën's celebrated designer Henri Chapron. ★ ☆ ☆ ☆ ☆

Corgi Oldsmobile Super 88, from
"The Man From U.N.C.L.E." television
series. ★ ☆ ☆ ☆ ☆

DINKY

The great Liverpudlian toymaker Frank Hornby – the man also responsible for Hornby railways and Meccano – came up with Dinky toys in 1931. Originally marketed as "Modelled Miniatures," the range was conceived as a companion to Hornby's railway sets. The name "Dinky" was used from 1934, and the toys were made at factories in Liverpool, England, and Bobigny, France. The models produced by the two factories often had subtle differences, particularly during the first years of production.

In order to survive in an increasingly competitive market, Dinky came up with a series of innovations that included treaded tires, fingertip steering, and "Speedwheels." Dinky also produced a wide range of film and television tie-ins alongside the more traditional scale models of real cars. The Dinky name is now owned by Universal.

Dinky 38B Talbot Sunbeam sports car; this is a late export issue of the model. ★ ★ ☆ ☆ ☆

Dinky 38 series Armstrong Siddeley coupé; a late export issue of this model. ★ ☆ ☆ ☆ ☆

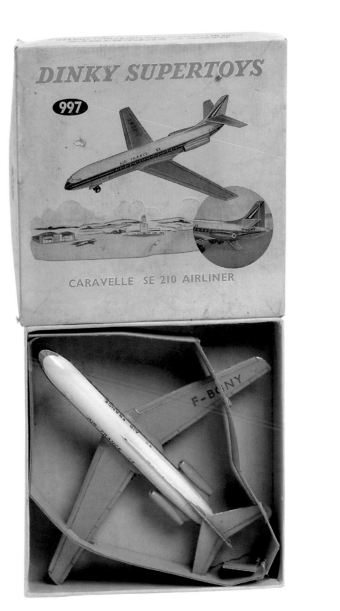

Dinky 997 Caravelle SE210 aircraft, in Air France livery, with metal wheels on undercarriage; has original box and packing strip. ★ ☆ ☆ ☆ ☆

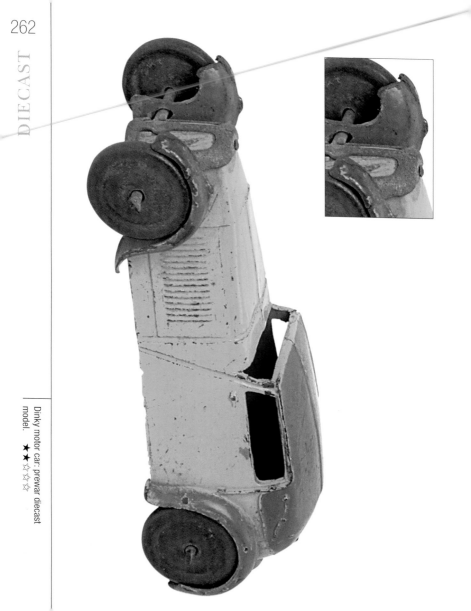

Dinky motor car: prewar diecast model. ★ ★ ☆ ☆ ☆

Dinky motor truck: prewar diecast model. ★ ☆ ☆ ☆

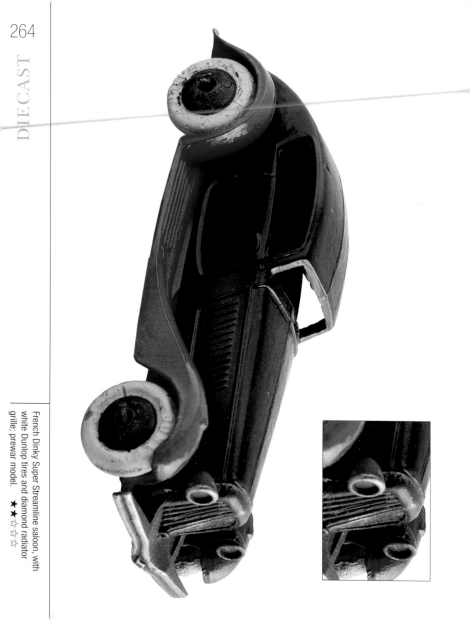

French Dinky Super Streamline saloon, with
white Dunlop tires and diamond radiator
grille; prewar model.   ★★☆☆☆

Dinky 30B Rolls Royce, with white tires; scarce prewar model.
1935–40 ★★ ☆☆☆

Dinky 104 Spectrum pursuit vehicle, as
seen in the animated television series
"Captain Scarlet." ★ ☆ ☆ ☆ ☆

Dynamic Action Features

DIRECT FROM

CAPTAIN SCARLET
AND THE
MYSTERONS

DINKY TOYS

SPV

Dinky 103 Spectrum patrol car, as seen in the animated television series "Captain Scarlet," has original box. ★ ☆☆☆☆

Dinky 131 Cadillac Eldorado, with driver figure; has original box. ★ ☆☆☆

Dinky 151 Triumph 1800 saloon car, in dark blue with light blue hubs; has original box. ★ ☆☆☆

Dinky 281 luxury coach, in cream, with orange flashes and cream hubs; has original box. ★☆☆☆☆

Dinky 161 Austin Somerset saloon car, in two-tone cream and black; has original box. ★ ★ ☆ ☆

Dinky 108 MG Midget sports car, with competition finish in red and tan and with driver figure; has original box. ★ ☆☆☆☆

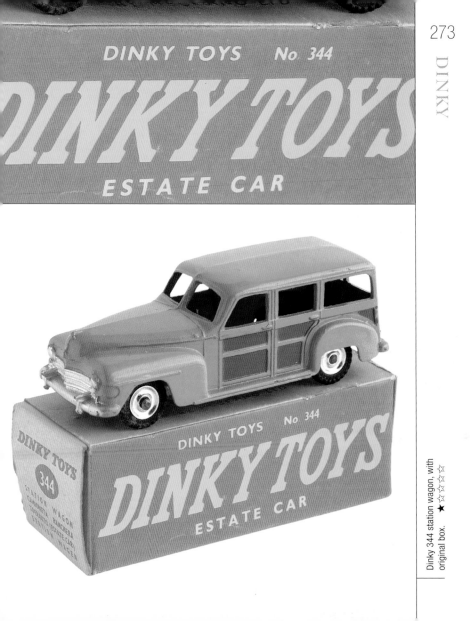

Dinky 344 station wagon, with original box. ★ ☆☆☆☆

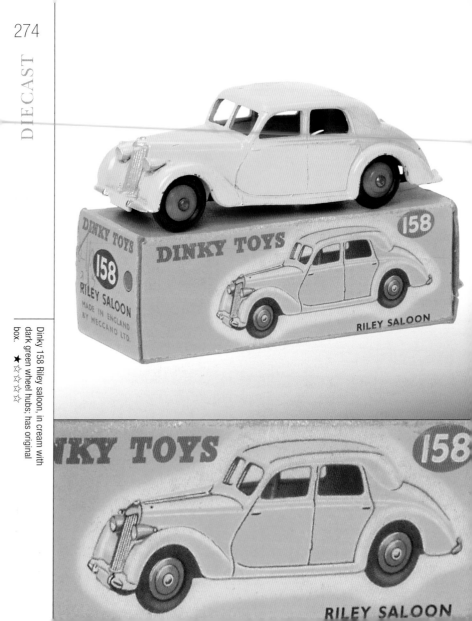

Dinky 158 Riley saloon, in cream with dark green wheel hubs; has original box. ★☆☆☆☆

Dinky 167 AC Aceca coupé, in light gray and red, with spun wheel hubs; has original box. ★ ☆☆☆

Dinky 168 Singer Gazelle, in two-tone green, with spun wheel hubs; has original box. ★ ☆☆☆

Dinky 100 Rolls Royce owned by Lady Penelope in the animated television series "Thunderbirds," equipped with missile and rocket. ★★☆☆☆

DINKY TOYS

100

LADY PENELOPE'S FAB 1

RADIATOR HINGES TO FIRE FORWARD ROCKET
FOUR REAR-FIRING HARPOONS
SLIDING COCKPIT CANOPY
LADY PENELOPE AND PARKER
JEWELLED HEADLIGHTS · PLATED DETAILS
SUSPENSION · NUMBER PLATES

DINKY

FAB

Lady **PENELOPE'S** FAB 1

Dinky 130 Ford Consul Corsair, in metallic red; has original box. ★ ☆ ☆ ☆ ☆

Dinky 257 Nash Rambler fire chief's car, with original box. ★ ☆ ☆ ☆ ☆

Dinky 157 Jaguar XK120 coupé in red, with original box. ★ ☆ ☆ ☆

Dinky 157 Jaguar XK120 coupé, in two-tone cerise and duck-egg blue; has original box. *1957–59* ★ ★ ★ ☆

Dinky 264 Royal Canadian Mounted Police Ford Fairlane, with police insignia; has original box. ★ ☆☆☆☆

Dinky 281 Pathe News camera car, with original box and instructions. ★ ☆ ☆ ☆

Dinky 191 Dodge Royal sedan, in light green with black flash; has original box. ★☆☆☆☆

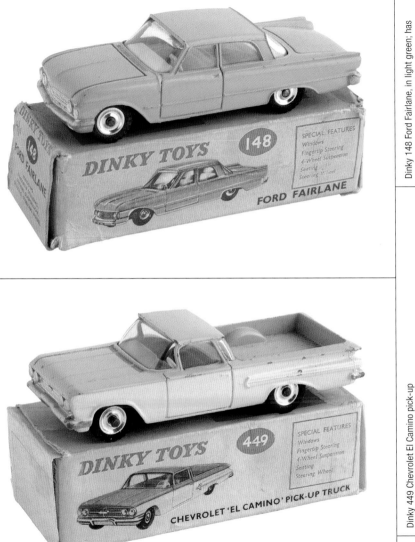

Dinky 148 Ford Fairlane, in light green; has original box. ★ ☆ ☆ ☆

Dinky 449 Chevrolet El Camino pick-up truck, in turquoise and cream; has original box. ★ ☆ ☆ ☆

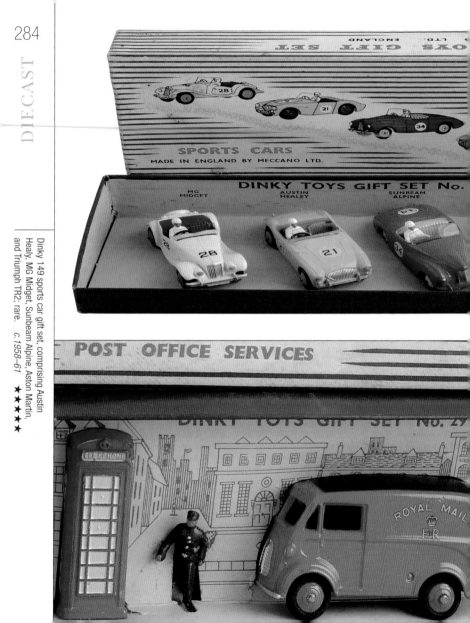

Dinky 149 sports car gift set, comprising Austin Healy, MG Midget, Sunbeam Alpine, Aston Martin, and Triumph TR2; rare. *c.1958–61* ★★★★★

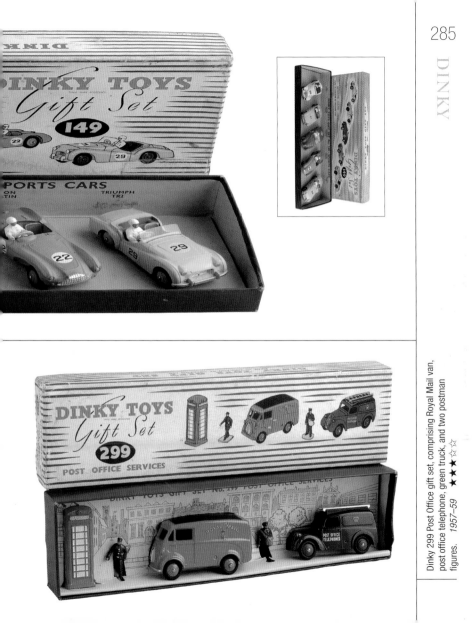

Dinky 299 Post Office gift set, comprising Royal Mail van, post office telephone, green truck, and two postman figures. *1957–59* ★ ★ ★ ☆ ☆

Dinky 2214 Ford Capri Rally Special, with racing number "12" decals; has original bubble pack. ★☆☆☆☆

Dinky 2162 Ford Capri, finished in metallic blue with black roof; has original bubble pack. ★ ☆ ☆ ☆

Dinky 255 Land Rover, in the livery of the Mersey Tunnel Police of Liverpool, England. *1955–60* ★ ☆ ☆ ☆ ☆

French Dinky 512 Kart midget racer, with driver figure, and with original box. ★ ★ ☆ ☆ ☆

Dinky Toys 106 Mini-Moke, from the television series "The Prisoner." A more valuable variation has spun wheel hubs pierced by the axles. *1967–70* ★★☆☆☆

Dinky Supertoys 562 dumper truck, with original box.   ★ ☆ ☆ ☆ ☆

Dinky motor truck: prewar diecast model. ★★☆☆☆

★★☆☆☆   Dinky motor truck: prewar diecast model.

DETAIL: Front of van, with "Ever Ready" logo above cab.

DINKY

Many toymakers used real-life cars as the inspiration for their models. This often meant emblazoning the names of famous companies on the sides of trucks, vans, and taxi cabs. Dinky embraced this practice so wholeheartedly that some collectors specialize in the firm's advertising vans. All sorts of products, from Ever Ready batteries to Spratt's dog food, found their way onto Dinky vans, and some of the rare variations can be very valuable. One example is the Dinky Big Bedford van in Heinz advertising livery that was made in the 1950s. The van came in two versions: one featuring a can of baked beans, and the other with a bottle of tomato ketchup. The ketchup bottle version was only produced for one year, and can be worth more than five times the price of the more common model with the baked bean can.

Dinky Supertoys 918 Guy van, in blue with red hubs and silver grille detail; has original box. ★ ★ ☆ ☆ ☆

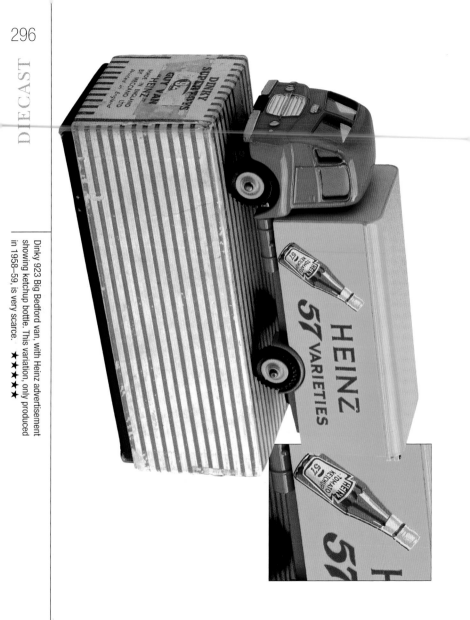

Dinky 923 Big Bedford van, with Heinz advertisement showing ketchup bottle. This variation, only produced in 1958–59, is very scarce. ★★★★★

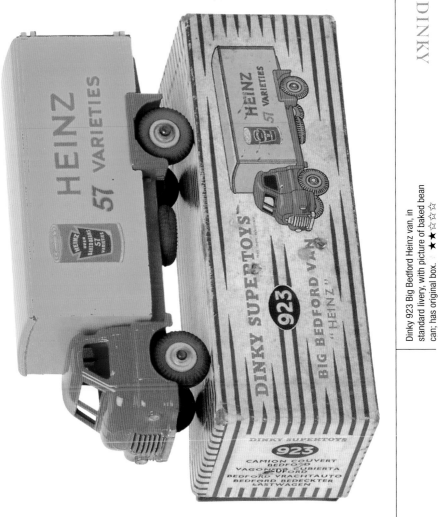

Dinky 923 Big Bedford Heinz van, in
standard livery, with picture of baked bean
can; has original box. ★ ★ ☆ ☆ ☆

Dinky 260 Royal Mail van, in
red with matt black roof, has
original box. ★ ★ ☆ ☆ ☆

DETAIL: Realistic Royal Mail insignia on side of van.

Dinky 481 Bedford CA van, with "Ovaltine" and "Ovaltine Biscuits" logos; has original box. ★☆☆☆☆

Dinky 450 Trojan van, in red, with "Esso" logo; has original box. ★ ☆☆☆☆

Dinky 452 Trojan van, with "Chivers Jellies" logo; has original box. ★ ☆☆☆☆

Dinky 917 Guy van, with red first type cab, cream body, and "Spratt's Bonio, Ovals & Dog Cakes" signs on sides; has original box.   ★★☆☆☆

Dinky 699 military vehicles gift set, comprising 674 Austin Champ, 641 cargo truck, 676 armored personnel carrier, and 621 heavy wagon; includes inner stand. ★★★☆☆

ARMOURED PERSONNEL CARRIER

3-TON ARMY WAGON

MILITARY VEHICLES (1)
MADE IN ENGLAND BY MECCANO LIMITED

Dinky Supertoys 956 Bedford turntable fire escape, with tinplate escape ladder; has original box. ★☆☆☆☆

Dinky Supertoys 958 Guy Warrior snow plow, with moveable plow blade; has original box. ★ ☆ ☆ ☆ ☆

Dinky 960 lorry-mounted cement mixer, with cement drum in blue and yellow; has original box. ★ ☆ ☆ ☆ ☆

Dinky 966 Marrel multi-bucket unit, in yellow with light gray painted skip; has original box. ★ ☆ ☆ ☆

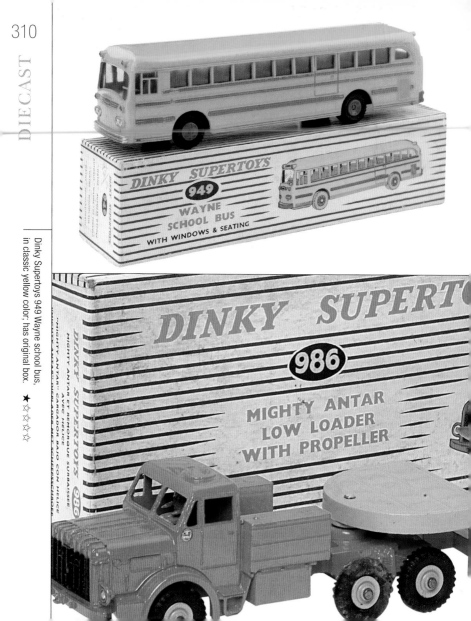

Dinky Supertoys 949 Wayne school bus, in classic yellow color; has original box. ★☆☆☆☆

Dinky Supertoys 986 Mighty Antar low loader with original Scimitar propeller cargo. The Antar was designed in 1949 for use in buiding oil pipelines. ★★☆☆☆

Dinky 942 Foden tanker, with blue second type cab, red wheels, tank, and "Regent" decals on sides: has original box. ★★☆☆☆

DINKY TOYS
TRADE MARK REGISTERED
905
FODEN FLAT TRUCK
WITH CHAINS

FODEN TRUCKS

Foden is among the oldest truck companies in the world, and the brand has had a loyal following for generations. The company was founded in 1856, during the age of steam, in Cheshire, England. From steam-powered trucks to diesel haulers and from coal wagons to cement mixers, toymakers have replicated Foden vehicles of all kinds over the years.

One of the most iconic Foden toys is the Dinky 505 Foden flatbed, first released in 1952. Many variations of this model exist – it was renumbered 905 in 1954 and output continued for a further ten years. Later versions can fetch upward of $180 (£100), but those from the first year of production – identifiable from a green or silver flash down the side of the cab – can be worth ten times that. Known as the "first type cab," these early trucks were made in green and maroon. Maroon is the more valuable – an example in pristine condition sold for £12,000 ($22,000) in 2003!

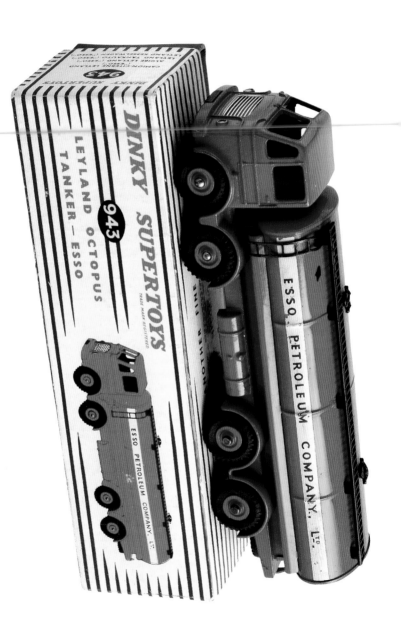

Dinky Supertoys 943 Leyland Octopus tanker, with ladder on top and with "Esso" decals; has original box. ★★☆☆☆

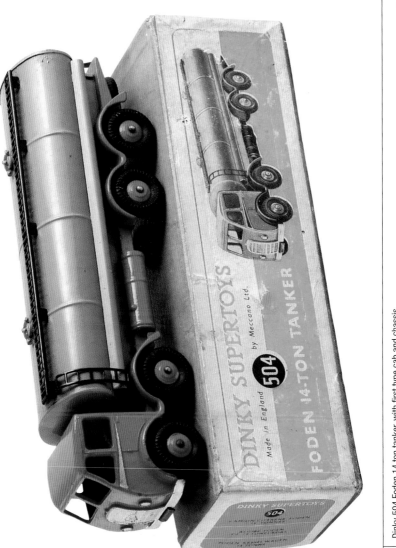

Dinky 504 Foden 14 ton tanker, with first type cab and chassis
in red; has original box. ★★★☆

Dinky 504 Foden 14 ton tanker; has first type cab in dark blue with light blue flash.   ★ ☆☆☆☆

Dinky 903 Foden flat truck, with dark blue cab, orange flatbed, and tailboard. ★ ☆ ☆ ☆ ☆

HEAVY DUTY

p.14

p.25

p.15

p.238

p.60

p.12

p.66

p.132

p.93

p.160

p.105

Dinky 521 Bedford articulated truck, in yellow with red hubs. ★ ☆ ☆ ☆ ☆

★ ☆ ☆ ☆

Dinky 522 Big Bedford truck, with maroon cab.

Dinky 905 Foden flatbed truck with chains; earlier versions, numbered 505, are generally more valuable. ★★☆☆☆

Dinky 505 Foden flatbed with chains; has original box. This is a rare maroon first type cab, produced only in 1952. ★★★★★

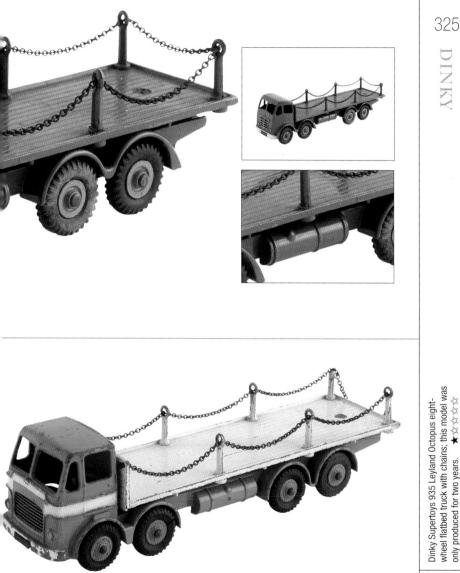

Dinky Supertoys 935 Leyland Octopus eight-wheel flatbed truck with chains; this model was only produced for two years. ★ ☆☆☆☆

Dinky Supertoys 979 Newmarket racehorse transport, with models of horses. *1961–64* ★ ☆☆☆☆

NEWMARKET RA
TRANSPORT SE

Dinky 280 observation coach: originally numbered 29F, renumbered 280 in 1954, and withdrawn in 1960. ★ ☆☆☆☆

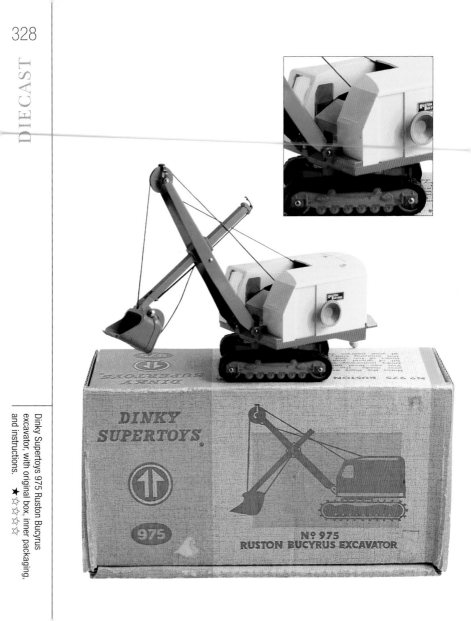

Dinky Supertoys 975 Ruston Bucyrus excavator, with original box, inner packaging, and instructions. ★☆☆☆☆

Dinky 945 AEC fuel tanker, with "Lucas Oil" decals; promotional model commissioned by Lucas Oil. Has original box. ★ ★ ☆ ☆

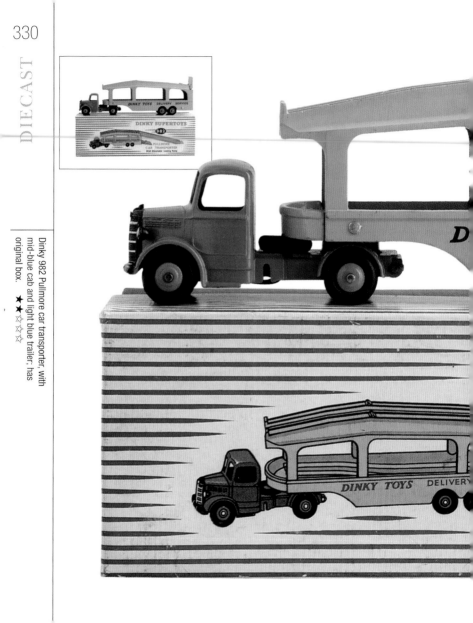

Dinky 982 Pullmore car transporter, with mid-blue cab and light blue trailer, has original box. ★★☆☆☆

Y TOYS   DELIVERY   SERVICE

DINKY SUPERTOYS

982

PULLMORE
CAR TRANSPORTER
With Detachable Loading Ramp

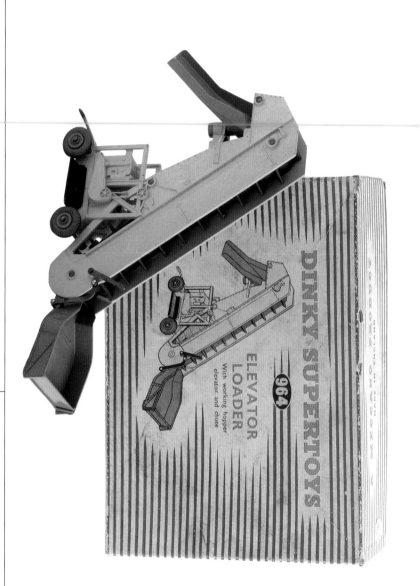

Dinky Supertoys 964 elevator loader, with original box. ★ ☆☆☆☆

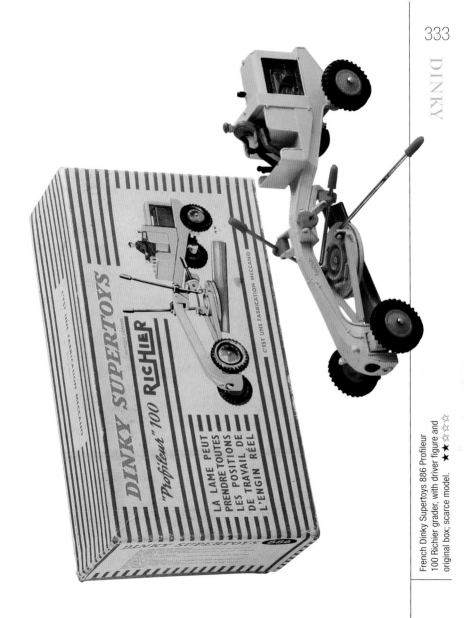

French Dinky Supertoys 886 Profileur
100 Richier grader, with driver figure and
original box; scarce model. ★ ★ ☆ ☆

French Dinky 577 Bataillere Berliet cattle wagon, with green and yellow plastic body and opening rear doors; has original box with picture. ★★★☆☆

DETAIL: Model comes with two cow figures.

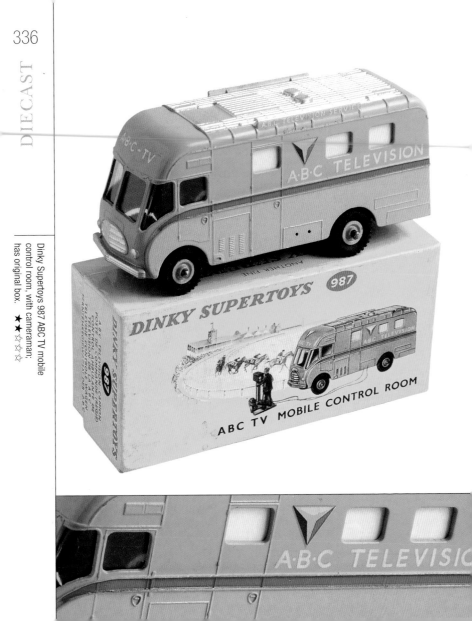

Dinky Supertoys 987 ABC TV mobile control room, with cameraman; has original box. ★★☆☆☆

Dinky Supertoys 988 ABC TV transmitter van, with detachable dish; has original box. ★ ☆☆☆☆

Dinky 968 BBC TV "Roving Eye" van in standard livery, with cameraman and aerial: has original box. ★ ☆☆☆☆

Dinky 969 BBC TV vehicle in standard livery, with extending mast and detachable dish; has original box and paperwork. ★ ☆☆☆☆

Dinky 671 Mk 1 Corvette high-speed warship with rocket launcher on aft deck: wooden prototype painted gray, cream, and white, with simple detailing. ★★☆☆☆

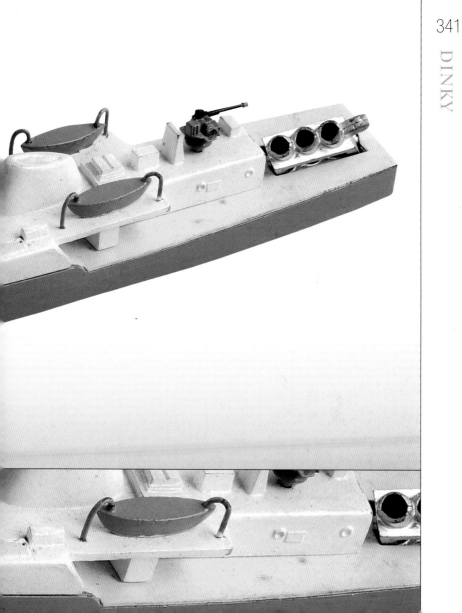

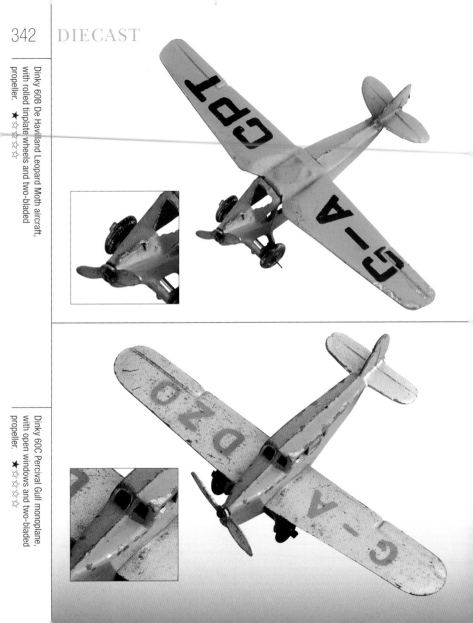

Dinky 60B De Havilland Leopard Moth aircraft, with rolled tinplate wheels and two-bladed propeller. ★☆☆☆☆

Dinky 60C Percival Gull monoplane, with open windows and two-bladed propeller. ★☆☆☆☆

Dinky 739 Zero Sen A6M5 fighter aircraft, with Japanese markings in red; has original bubble pack. ★ ☆ ☆ ☆

Dinky 721 Junkers JU 87B Stuka with bomb, in dark green with pale blue underside; has original box and packaging. ★☆☆☆☆

Direct from the epic film

"Battle of Britain"

DINKY TOYS ®

WITH DROPPING CAP-FIRING BOMB!

Caps not supplied

1ST AGAIN

© Spitfire Productions Ltd. 1969

JUNKERS Ju 87B

STUKA

DETAIL: First-issue box; tie-in with the 1969 film "Battle of Britain."

Dinky 719 Mark II Spitfire in RAF camouflage livery, from the film "Battle of Britain," has original box and packaging. ★★☆☆☆

Direct from the epic film

"Battle of Britain"

DINKY TOYS ®

SPITFIRE Mk II

1ST GEAR

MOTOR DRIVEN
PROPELLER

Battery (Sales No. 035) not supplied.

Retractable Undercarriage

© Spitfire Productions Ltd. 1969

DETAIL: First-issue box, showing tie-in with film.

DETAIL: Hand-painted, dark green camouflage patches.

PROTOTYPES

Any new model must undergo a lengthy development process before a toy company will commit resources to its production. Initial ideas will usually take the form of photographs or sketches. These are used to create the first three-dimensional prototype, which is often hand-carved in wax. Further prototypes are constructed at every stage of development, to evaluate changes, assess color, and check the suitability of the final molds for the casting process.

There are a number of reasons why collectors covet prototypes. Many of them, particularly those used to create master molds, are modeled to a very high standard. Some prototypes feature colors or aspects of design that were never put into general production. The cachet that comes with owning a piece of a famous toy's history only adds to the allure of these special items.

Dinky prototype diecast Phantom II F-4K aircraft in light gray. The production version of this model was made only in navy blue. ★ ★ ☆ ☆ ☆

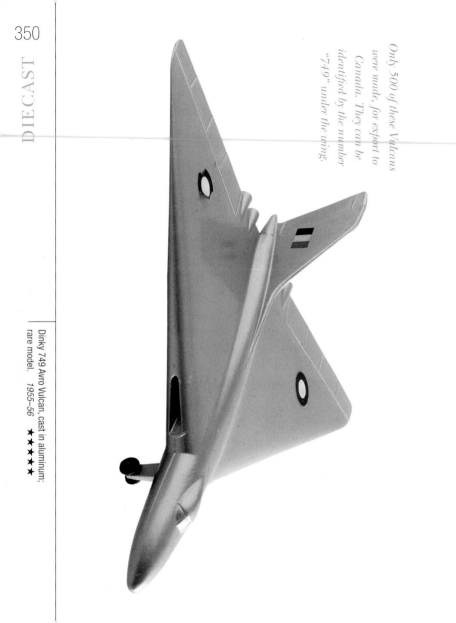

Only 500 of these Vulcans were made, for export to Canada. They can be identified by the number "749" under the wing.

Dinky 749 Avro Vulcan, cast in aluminum; rare model. 1955–56 ★★★★★

French Dinky 60F SE Caravelle, in white
and silver Air France livery; has original
box and paperwork. ★★☆☆☆

HOT WHEELS®

Mattel's Hot Wheels® range raced onto the diecast car market in 1968. Fantasy hot rods such as the "Silhouette" were issued side-by-side with customized versions of American classics such as the Pontiac Firebird. The runaway success of the first 16 models led to rapid expansion of the line, and more than 100 models were available by 1971.

The 1981 "Hot Ones" range was touted as the fastest on the market, only to be succeeded by the even speedier "Ultra Hots" in 1984. "Hi-Rakers," launched in 1980, featured an adjustable rear axle for that genuine dragster look. Sponsorship of events such as NASCAR has assured the brand's association with extreme speed. The 2 billionth Hot Wheels® car was cast in 1998 and a Hot Wheels® film is currently in production.

Hot Wheels® 6261 Spittin' Image,
in orange, with decal on hood.
1969 ★ ☆☆☆☆☆

Hot Wheels® 6253 classic 1936 Ford coupé, in pink. This color was initially referred to as "lavender." *1969* ★★☆☆☆

★ ☆ ☆ ☆ ☆

1970

Hot Wheels® 6413 Seasider, in metallic yellow.

DIECAST

Hot Wheels® 6220 custom Volkswagen, in red. *1968* ★ ☆ ☆ ☆ ☆

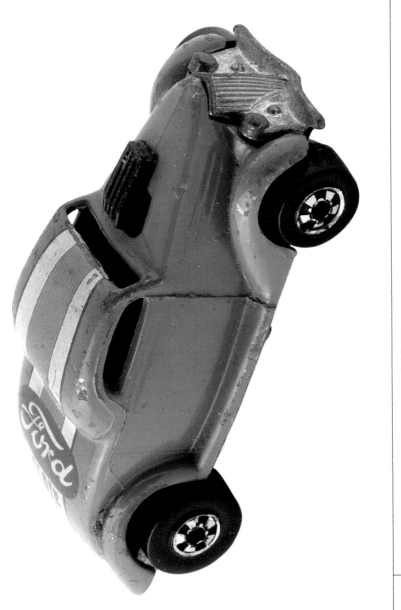

★ ☆☆☆☆

1976 Hot Wheels® 9244 Neet Streeter, in blue.

Hot Wheels® 6219 Hot Heap, in purple. *1968* ★☆☆☆☆

Hot Wheels® 6250 "Redline" classic 1932 Ford Vicky, in blue. *1969* ★☆☆☆☆

Hot Wheels® 6402 Paddy Wagon, with "Police" marked
on rear of cab. *1970* ★ ☆☆☆☆

SPEED TESTS

When Mattel launched the Hot Wheels® range in 1968, such was its success that other toy companies were forced to sit up and take notice. Mattel's engineers had realized that tapered wheels attached to a very thin axle could reduce friction, producing cars that rolled faster. Hubs made from Delrin – a patent plastic resin – gave each wheel independent suspension and made the cars even speedier.

Hot Wheels® left their competitors eating dust, but not for long. The first Matchbox® toys with "Superfast® Wheels" were released in 1969, along with Corgi's "Whizz Wheels" range. Moreover, Dinky came up with "Speed Wheels." Unfortunately, no test yet devised has satisfactorily proved which wheels really are the fastest; it's just too close to call.

Hot Wheels® 1475 Corvette Stingray, in silver. 1979 ★ ☆ ☆ ☆ ☆

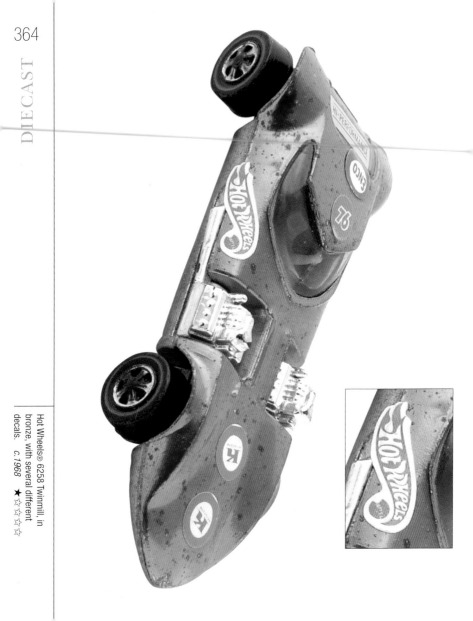

Hot Wheels® 6258 Twinmill, in bronze, with several different decals. *c.1968* ★☆☆☆☆

Hot Wheels® 6188 Striptease, in turquoise, with exposed engine block and various decals.   *c.1970*   ★ ☆ ☆ ☆ ☆

Hot Wheels® 2012 Jaguar XJS, in
metallic gold, with Jaguar decals on
sides. *1978* ★ ☆ ☆ ☆ ☆

Hot Wheels® 6196 Mercedes Benz
C111, in red, with decals and plastic
baseplate.   *1972*   ★ ☆ ☆ ☆ ☆

Hot Wheels® 2014 Hotbird, in black, with decal on hood. *1978* ★☆☆☆☆

Hot Wheels® 3255 Datsun 200 SX, in gold, with "200 SX" decal to side.   *1983*   ★ ☆☆☆☆

Hot Wheels® 6205 custom Cougar, in
green. *1968* ★ ☆☆☆☆

Hot Wheels® 2013 1957 Thunderbird, in yellow. *1978* ★ ☆ ☆ ☆ ☆

Hot Wheels® 6212 custom Firebird, in green,
with decals on doors and trunk.   *1968*   ★ ☆☆ ☆☆

Hot Wheels® 6176 Short Order, in yellow.
1971 ★ ☆☆☆☆

Hot Wheels® 6423 Mantis, in green, with racing number "4." *1970* ★☆☆☆☆

Hot Wheels® 6029 Silhouette, in metallic green, with painted base. *1968* ★ ☆ ☆ ☆ ☆

HIGH PERFORMANCE

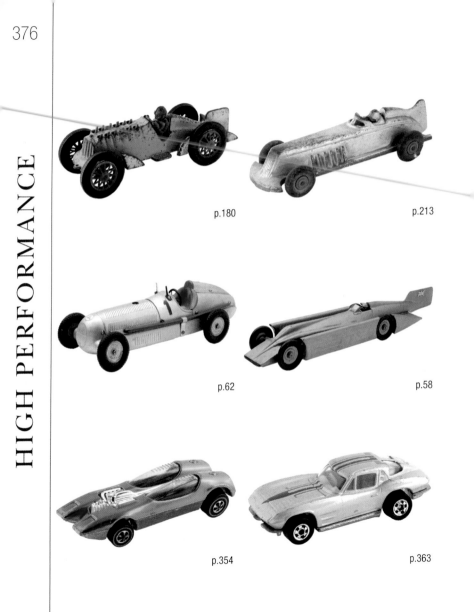

p.180

p.213

p.62

p.58

p.354

p.363

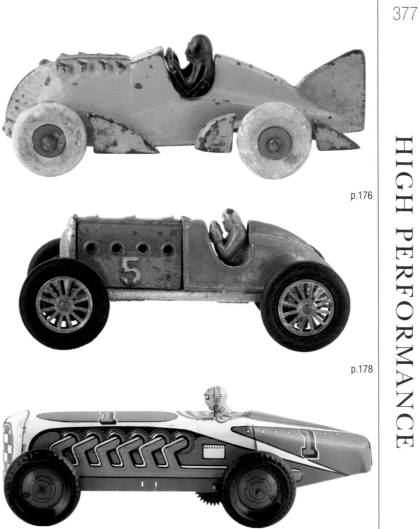

p.176

p.178

p.69

Hot Wheels® 8272 Large Charge, in green, with lightning-strike decals. *1975* ★☆☆☆☆

Hot Wheels® 6266 custom Continental
Mark III, in purple.   *1969*   ★ ☆☆☆☆

Hot Wheels® 6213 custom Fleetside, in purple, with decals on doors. *1967* ★ ☆ ☆ ☆ ☆

Hot Wheels® 6210 Deora, in metallic blue.
1968 ★ ☆ ☆ ☆ ☆

Hot Wheels® 6274 Volkswagen
Beachbomb, with surfboards tucked into
racks at sides.   *1969*   ★ ☆ ☆ ☆ ☆

Hot Wheels® 7666 Ranger Rig, in green, with "Forest Service" decals on doors. *1975* ★☆☆☆

Hot Wheels® 6410 Mongoose Funny Car, in electric blue. *1970* ★☆☆☆☆

Hot Wheels® 7621 Funny Money; a combination
of a heavy truck with Hot Wheels® cars' trademark
"Funny Car." *1974* ★ ☆ ☆ ☆ ☆

DIECAST

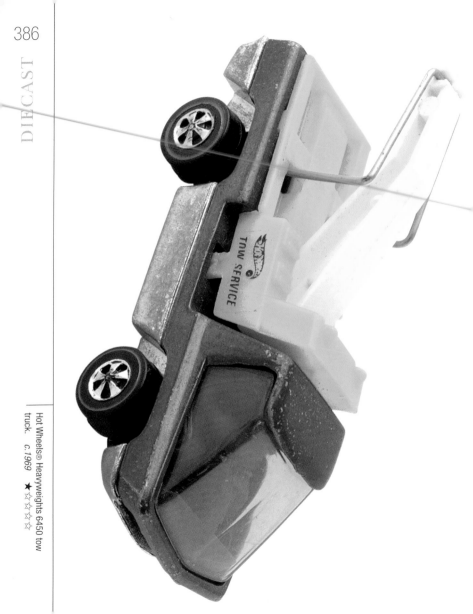

Hot Wheels® Heavyweights 6450 tow truck. *c.1969* ★ ☆☆☆☆

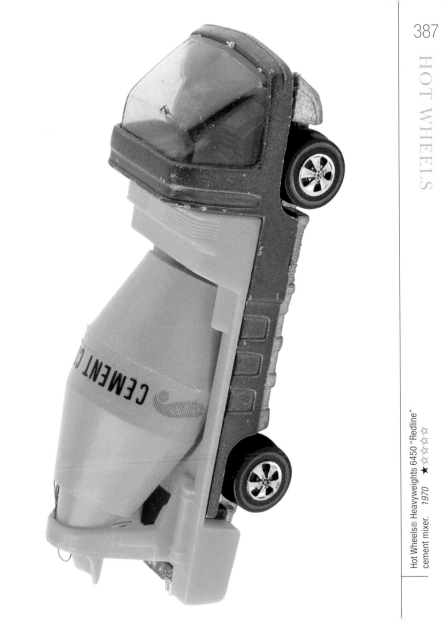

CEMENT C

Hot Wheels® Heavyweights 6450 "Redline"
cement mixer. *1970* ★ ☆ ☆ ☆

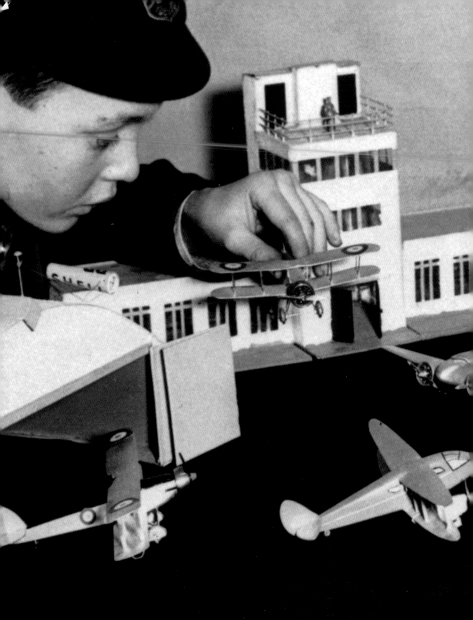

OTHER
DIECAST

Diecast toys were made possible by the invention of the
Linotype machine, designed by Ottmar Mergenthaler in
1886 for the printing industry. The smoother finish and
greater accuracy offered by die-casting led to its rapid
domination of the toy industry. The first diecast car was
a Model T Ford produced by Charles Dowst, founder of
Tootsietoy, in 1906. Following the American lead, firms
such as Solido in France and Lesney in England began to
make diecast vehicles.

The level of detail made possible by die-casting was
particularly useful for creating miniature models of famous
road cars, ocean liners and aircraft. The dies used to create
this new generation of toys were
valuable commodities and were
sometimes used by more than
one company.

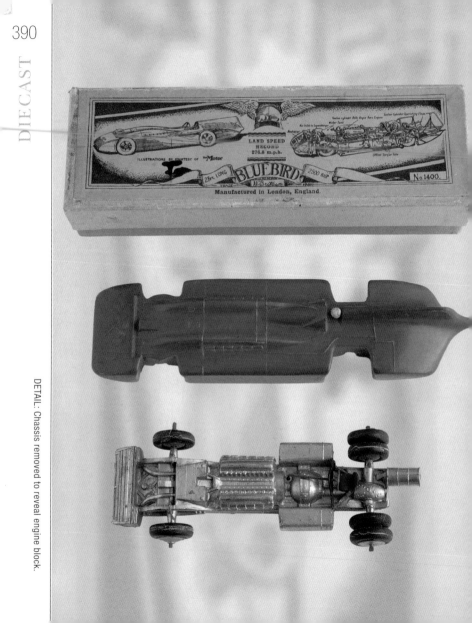

DETAIL: Chassis removed to reveal engine block.

BRITAINS

William Britain began producing toys in 1893. For more than 70 years, Britains was a leading manufacturer of cast metal toys, becoming particularly well known for detailed sets of lead soldiers depicting regiments from different armies in the world. At certain points in the company's long history, however, particularly in the aftermath of the First World War, there was a diminished public appetite for soldiers and guns. The company's solution was to develop a range of farm vehicles. Later, they produced toys featuring famous characters, or which were linked to events such as Sir Malcolm Campbell's breaking of the land speed record in 1935, when he exceeded 300mph (482kph) for the first time. While representing only a small proportion of the firm's output, Britains diecast vehicles have a reputation for high quality and fine detailing that ensures continued interest from collectors.

Britains 1400 Bluebird, modeled on the first car to exceed 300mph. Has original labeled box; rare. ★★☆☆☆

Britains 1433 caterpillar-type, covered military wagon, with hinged tailboard, tow hook, driver figure, and light brown tinplate cover; has original box. ★★☆☆☆

BRITAINS MILITARY EQUIPMENT

Covered Tender
(With Driver)

Caterpillar Type   Back drops

OIL THE WORKING PARTS OCCASIONALLY

MANUFACTURED BY   *W.Britain*   IN LONDON ENGLAND

TRADE   REGD No 459993   MARK

Y EQUIPMENT

overed Tender
(With Driver)

rpillar Type   Back drops

THE WORKING PARTS OCCASIONALLY

ACTURED BY   *W.Britain*   IN LONDON ENGLAND

ADE   REGD No 459993   MARK

CIJ Renault Colorale van, with spun white metal wheels; has original box. ★ ☆ ☆ ☆ ☆

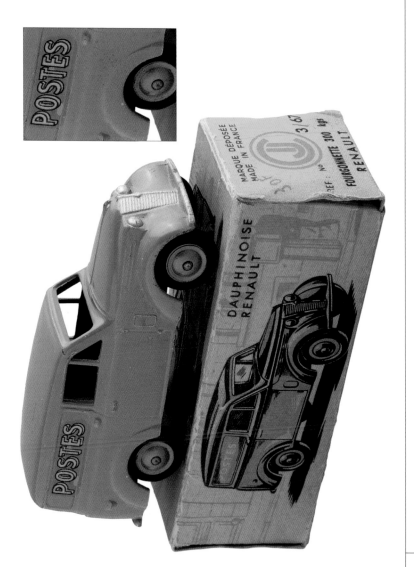

CIJ Renault Dauphinoise post van,
with "Postes" yellow decals on side;
has original box. ★ ☆ ☆ ☆

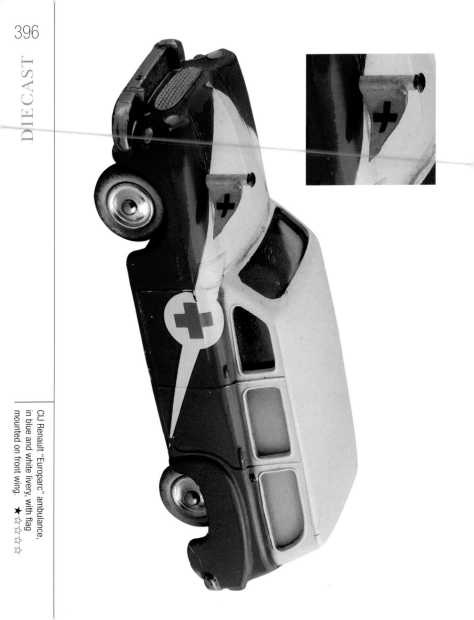

CIJ Renault "Europarc" ambulance, in blue and white livery, with flag mounted on front wing. ★☆☆☆☆

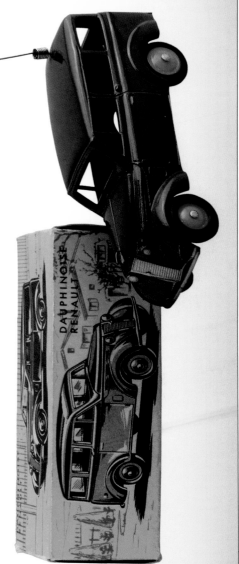

CIJ Renault Dauphinoise Gendarmerie van, with windows and roof aerial; has original box. ★ ☆☆☆☆

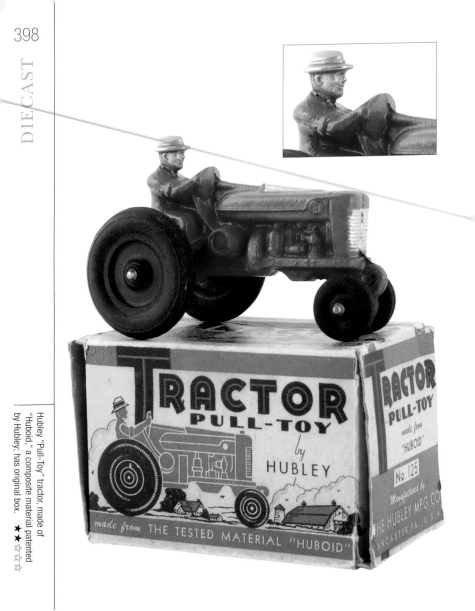

Hubley "Pull-Toy" tractor, made of "Huboid," a composite material patented by Hubley; has original box. ★★☆☆☆

Hubley diecast tractor, with nickel driver and "Indiana State Fair" label on hood; has original box. ★ ☆☆☆☆

Hubley diecast MG open roadster, with embossed seating and grille and spare tire; has original box. ★★☆☆☆

Small motorcycle with rider figure and rubber tires, in the style of Hubley. ★★☆☆☆

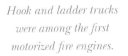

*Hook and ladder trucks
were among the first
motorized fire engines.*

Hubley die cast hook and ladder truck, with nickel-plated ladder supports, three cast iron ladders, and driver figure. ★ ★ ★ ☆ ☆

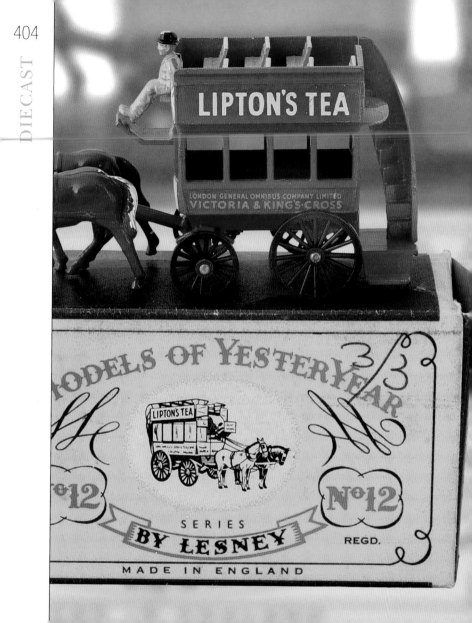

LIPTON'S TEA

LONDON GENERAL OMNIBUS COMPANY LIMITED
VICTORIA & KING'S CROSS

MODELS OF YESTERYEAR

LIPTONS TEA

No 12

No 12

SERIES

BY LESNEY

REGD.

MADE IN ENGLAND

MODELS OF YESTERYEAR®

Leslie and Rodney Smith founded Lesney in 1947. Shortly afterwards, they were joined at the converted pub that served as their headquarters by a modeler called Jack Odell. His "Models of Yesteryear®" range was launched at the Harrogate Toy Fair in 1956. There were 16 vehicles in the first series, which was produced until 1960; the vintage omnibuses and Allchin traction engines appealed to both children and adult enthusiasts. Thereafter, Lesney replaced older models with new issues, including European and American cars. Many collectors regard this second series as the cream of Lesney's output. The "Models of Yesteryear®" range was sidelined in 1969, when resources were diverted to the "Superfast® Wheels" project. Jack Odell retired in 1973.

Lesney "Models of Yesteryear®" horse-drawn bus, with "Lipton's Tea" advertising sign. 1959 ★ ☆☆☆☆

Matchbox® Series 56 London trolleybus, with metal wheels; has original box. Variation with gray plastic wheels is rarer and more valuable. *c. 1960* ★★☆☆☆

MICA stands for Matchbox International Collector's Association.

Y-5/42

"Models of Yesteryear®" MICA Leyland Titan double-decker bus. ★ ☆☆☆☆

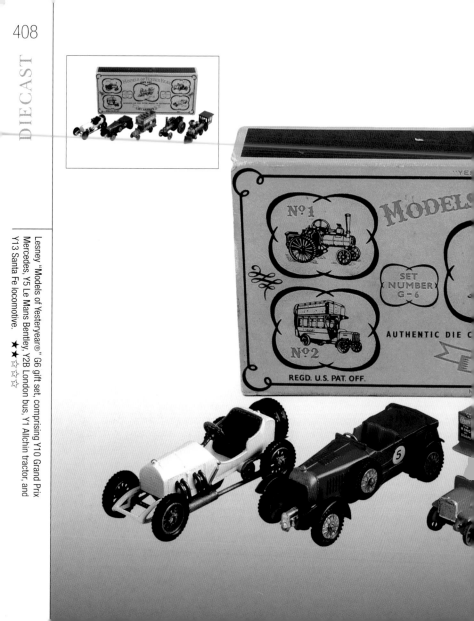

Lesney "Models of Yesteryear®" G6 gift set, comprising Y10 Grand Prix Mercedes, Y5 Le Mans Bentley, Y2B London bus, Y1 Allchin tractor, and Y13 Santa Fe locomotive. ★★☆☆☆

Matchbox® MB17 Bedford removals van, with "Matchbox Removals Service" livery and metal wheels. ★☆☆☆☆

Lesney 745D Massey Harris tractor, with gold detailing and steerable front axle; early model. *c.1955* ★ ★ ☆ ☆ ☆

Matchbox® Superfast® 32C Leyland oil tanker, with original box; "National Association of Matchbox Collectors" transfer increases value by about 30 percent. *1970–73* ★★☆☆☆

Matchbox® Series 22 Vauxhall Cresta, in pink. ★ ☆☆☆☆

Matchbox® Superkings® Caravelle caravan. ★ ☆☆☆

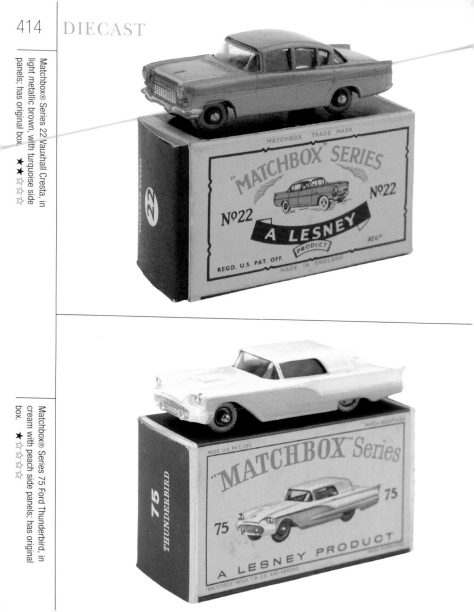

Matchbox® Series 22 Vauxhall Cresta, in light metallic brown, with turquoise side panels; has original box. ★★☆☆☆

Matchbox® Series 75 Ford Thunderbird, in cream with peach side panels; has original box. ★☆☆☆☆

Matchbox® Series 22 Vauxhall Cresta, in pale gray with lilac side panels; has original box. ★ ☆ ☆ ☆ ☆

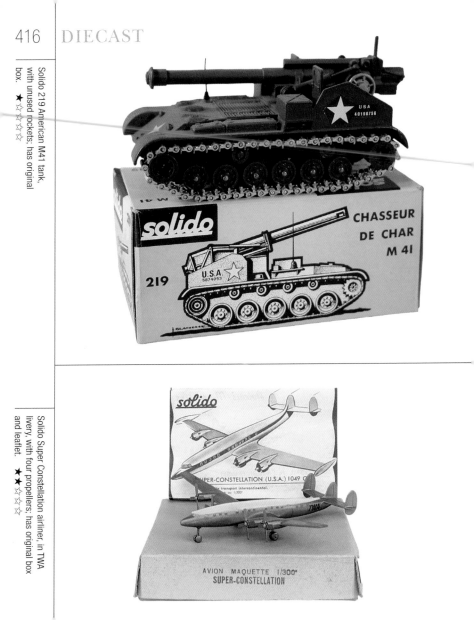

Solido 219 American M41 tank, with unused rockets; has original box. ★☆☆☆☆

Solido Super Constellation airliner, in TWA livery, with four propellers; has original box and leaflet. ★★☆☆☆

Solido Age d'Or Bugatti Royale, in dark blue, with original box and accessories. ★ ☆☆☆☆

Solido James Bond "Goldfinger" Rolls Royce, from a limited edition of 100, with Goldfinger and Oddjob figures. ★★★ ☆☆

TEKNO

Tekno was founded near Copenhagen, Denmark in 1928 by A. Siegumfeldt, a self-employed plumber. The firm grew to become one of Europe's largest toymakers, exporting hundreds of thousands of models around the world each year. In its early years, the company received a boost when it won a prestigious award from the Federation of Danish Industries. During the 1940s, occupying Nazi forces imposed harsh restrictions on Danish industry, even arresting Siegumfeldt for producing model aircraft. Tekno survived, however, expanding throughout the 1950s and 1960s. Financial problems in the early 1970s led to bankruptcy, and the Danish operations were closed down. The company still survives in the Netherlands, producing collector's-edition models of trucks in haulage company liveries.

Tekno 415 Taunus transit ambulance, with decals on sides, blue roof light, and figure on stretcher; has original box. ★ ☆ ☆ ☆ ☆

Tekno 415 Taunus transit van, with "Falck Zonen" decals (representing Denmark's combined fire service, formed in 1963) on sides. ★☆☆☆☆

Tekno 419 Ford Taunus Solgryn van, with original box. Solgryn is a popular Danish brand of oatmeal. ★ ★ ★ ☆ ☆

Tekno LP322 Mercedes Benz "Kosangas" gas truck, with gas bottles and sack barrow; has original box. ★ ★ ☆ ☆ ☆

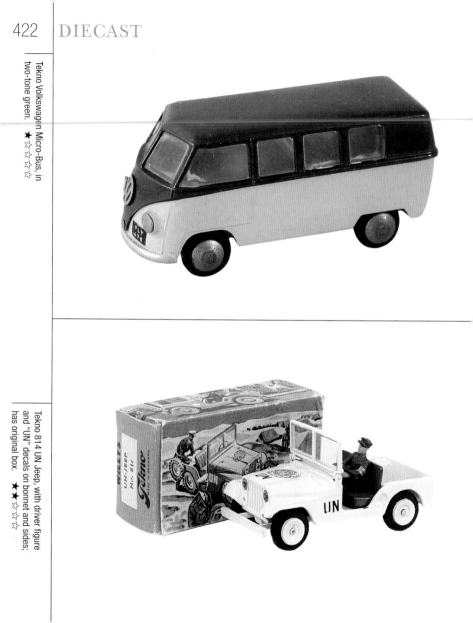

Tekno Volkswagen Micro-Bus, in two-tone green. ★☆☆☆☆

Tekno 814 UN Jeep, with driver figure and "UN" decals on bonnet and sides; has original box. ★★☆☆☆

Tekno 815 caravan, with folding drawbar and registration transfer; scarce model. ★ ☆☆☆☆

Tekno 834R Mustang rally car, with "169" racing number decal; has original box. ★ ☆☆☆☆

DIECAST

"Any parent who has ever found a rusted toy automobile buried in the grass ... knows that objects like these can be among the most powerful things in the world."

SPORTS ILLUSTRATED

Tootsie prewar Ford Tri-Motor aircraft, in silver, with three propellers and white rubber tires. ★★☆☆☆

Tootsie town car, in blue, with rubber tires, metallic grille, and spare tire. ★★★☆

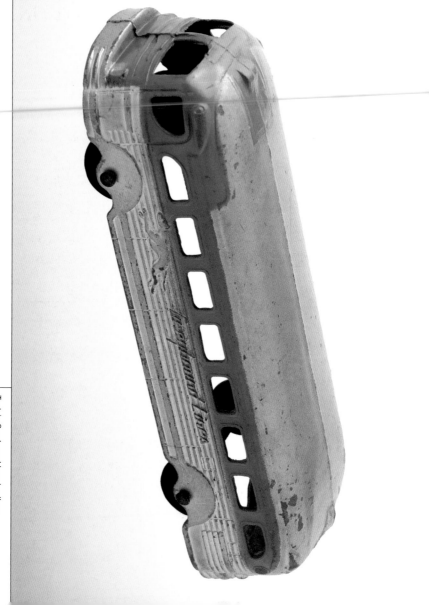

Tootsie Greyhound bus, in silver and blue livery.   ★☆☆☆☆

Tri-Ang Spot-On Austin 7 Mini, in light gray with red interior; scarce model. ★ ★ ☆ ☆ ☆

Tri-Ang Spot-On 185 Fiat 500, in light gray with cream interior; has original box. *1963* ★ ☆ ☆ ☆ ☆

DETAIL: Model finished in pink, with cream interior.

TRI-ANG SPOT-ON

In just eight years, from 1959 to 1967, Tri-Ang produced a range of more than 100 model vehicles as part of its Spot-On range. The company manufactured the range at factories in Ireland and New Zealand. As the name suggests, Spot-On was Tri-Ang's attempt to create a line of toys that all shared the same accurate scale and attention to detail. Every Tri-Ang Spot-On model has a uniform scale of 1:42, unlike many other brands, which used smaller scales for larger vehicles. The "Tommy Spot" gift sets came with boxes that doubled as play scenes, such as garages, high streets, and house fronts. Spot-On vehicles can be hard to source as they were relatively expensive when first sold. Examples in mint or excellent condition and in their original boxes can sell for large sums today.

Tri-Ang Spot-On 166 Renault Floride, with original box and instruction leaflet. ★ ★ ☆ ☆ ☆

Tri-Ang Spot-On 118 BMW Isetta, with original box; yellow variation can be worth up to 30 percent more. ★ ☆☆☆☆

Tri-Ang Spot-On 131 Goggomobile, in pink with cream interior; has original box. ★ ☆☆☆☆

Tri-Ang Spot-On 119 Meadows Frisky, in pale green with black roof and cream interior; has original box. ★ ☆☆☆☆

Tri-Ang Spot-On 100 Ford Zodiac, in lilac with cream interior; has original box and instruction leaflet. ★ ☆☆☆

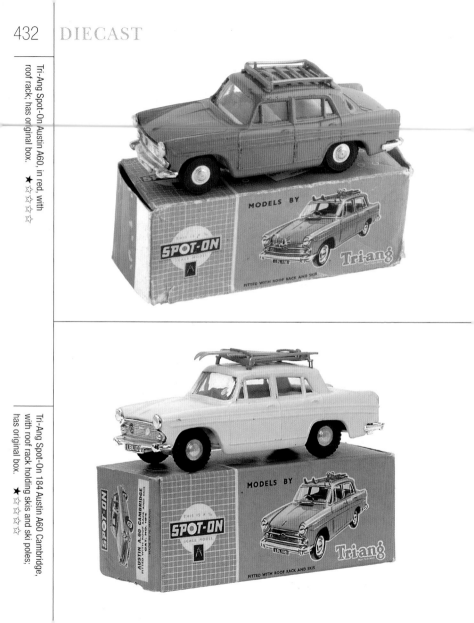

Tri-Ang Spot-On Austin A60, in red, with roof rack; has original box. ★ ☆☆☆☆

Tri-Ang Spot-On 184 Austin A60 Cambridge, with roof rack holding skis and ski poles; has original box. ★ ☆☆☆☆

Tri-Ang Spot-On 161 LWB Land Rover, with spare tire on bonnet; has original box. ★ ☆☆☆☆

Tri-Ang Spot-On 213 Ford Anglia, in red with cream interior; has original box. ★★☆☆☆

Tri-Ang Spot-On 120 Fiat Multipla, in pale blue with white interior; has original box. ★☆☆☆☆

Tri-Ang Spot-On 193 NSU Prinz 4, with driver figure; has original box. *1963* ★☆☆☆☆

Tri-Ang Spot-On 154 Austin A40, in lilac with black roof and cream interior; has original box. *1961* ★ ☆☆☆☆

Tri-Ang Spot-On 115 Bristol 406, in metallic blue with cream interior; has original box. ★★ ☆☆☆

VACATIONS & TRAVEL

p.134

p.71

p.35

p.382

p.70

p.140

p.13

p.56

p.423

p.422

p.413

VACATIONS & TRAVEL

Benbros Motor Cycle Rally Rider, with rubber tires and detachable rider; has original box with period illustration. ★ ☆☆☆☆

USING THE INTERNET

★ The internet has revolutionized the trading of collectibles as it provides a cost-effective way of buying and selling, away from the overheads of shops and auction rooms. Many millions of collectibles are offered for sale and traded daily, with sites varying from global online marketplaces, such as eBay, to specialist dealers' websites.

★ When searching online, remember that some people may not know how to accurately describe their item. General category searches, even though more time consuming, and even purposefully misspelling a name, can yield results. Also, if something looks too good to be true, it probably is. Using this book to get to know your market visually, so that you can tell the difference between a real bargain and something that sounds like one, is a good start.

★ As you will understand from buying this book, color photography is vital – look for online listings that include as many images as possible and check them carefully. Beware that colors can appear differently, even between computer screens.

★ Always ask the vendor questions about the object, particularly regarding condition. If there is no image, or you want to see another aspect of the object – ask. Most sellers (private or trade) will want to realize the best price for their items so will be more than happy to help – if approached politely and sensibly.

★ As well as the "e-hammer" price, you will probably have to pay additional transactional fees such as packing, shipping, and possibly regional or national taxes. It is always best to ask for an estimate of these additional costs before leaving a bid. This will also help you tailor your bid as you will have an idea of the maximum price the item will cost if you are successful.

★ As well as the well-known online auction sites, such as eBay, there is a host of other online resources for buying and selling, for example fair and auction date listings.

MUSEUMS

Australia

**New South Wales Toy
& Railway Museum**
36 Olympian Parade
Leura
NSW 2780
Tel: 02 4784 1169
Fax: 02 4784 2462

Australian Toy Museum
180 Smith Street
Collingwood
VIC 3066
Tel: 03 9419 4138

France

Musée du Jouet
1, Enclos de l'Abbaye
78300 Poissy
Tel: 01 39 65 06 06
Fax: 01 39 65 03 14

Germany

**Spielzeugmuseum Nürnberg
(Nuremberg Toy Museum)**
Karlstrasse 13–15
90403 Nuremberg
Tel: 911 231 3164
Fax: 911 231 2710
email: spielzeugmuseum@stadt.
nuernberg.de
web: www.spielzeugmuseum-
nuernberg.de/

Japan

Japan Toy Museum
671-3 Nakanino Kodera-cho
Kanzaki-gun Hyogo 679-2143
Tel: 0792 32 4388
Fax: 0792 32 7174
e-mail: info@japan-toy-museum.org
web: www.japan-toy-museum.org

South Africa

Stellenbosch Museum
Erfurthuis
Ryneveldstreet 37
Stellenbosch 7600
Tel: 021 887 2948
email: stelmus@mweb.co.za
web: www.museums.org.za/stellmus/

UK

**The Brighton Toy
and Model Museum**
52–55 Trafalgar Street
Brighton
Sussex BN1 4EB
Tel: 01273 749 494
email: info123@brightontoymuseum.
co.uk
web: www.brightontoymuseum.co.uk/

**Victoria & Albert Museum
of Childhood**
Cambridge Heath Road
London E2 9PA
Tel: 0208 983 5200
web: www.vam.ac.uk/moc/

USA

The Official Marx Toy Museum
915 Second Street
Moundsville
WV 26041
Tel: 304 845-6022
email: museum@marxtoymuseum.
com
web: www.marxtoymuseum.com/

World's Largest Toy Museum
3609 West Highway 76
Branson
MO 65616
Tel: 417 332 1499
Fax: 417 332 0017
email: torwbeck@inter-linc.net
web: www.worldslargesttoymuseum.
com

The Toy Museum
Frank L. Horton Museum Center
924 South Main Street
Winston-Salem
NC 27101
Tel: 336 721 7300
web: www.oldsalem.org

Hot Wheels® Hall of Fame
Petersen Automotive Museum
6060 Wilshire Boulevard
Los Angeles
CA 90036
Tel: 323 930 2277
web: www.petersen.org/

**Smithsonian National Museum
of American History**
Behring Centre
National Mall, 14th Street
and Constitution Avenue, N.W
Washington D.C.
Tel: 202 633 1000
email: info@si.edu
web: americanhistory.si.edu

**The Toy Museum at
Natural Bridge of Virginia**
PO Box 87
Natural Bridge
VA 24578
Tel: 540 291 9920
email: info@awesometoymuseum.com
web: www.awesometoymuseum.com

DEALERS AND AUCTION HOUSES

Atomic Age
318 East Virginia Road,
Fulleron, CA 92831 USA
Tel: 001 714 446 0736
Fax: 001 714 446 0436

Auction Team Köln
Postfach 50 11 19, Bonner
Str. 528-530, D-50971
Cologne, Germany
Tel: 00 49 221 38 70 49
auction@breker.com
www.breker.com

Auktionshaus Kaup
Schloss Sulzburg,
Hauptstrasse 62,
79295 Sulzburg, Germany
Tel: 0049 7634 5038 0
www.kaupp.de

Bertoia Auctions
2141 Demarco Drive,
Vineland NJ 08360 USA
Tel: 001 856 692 1881
toys@BertoiaAuctions.com
www.bertoiaauctions.com

**Black Horse
Antique Showcase**
2222 North Reading Road,
Denver PA, 17517 USA
Tel: 001 717 335 3300
www.antiques-showcase.
com

**Bucks County
Antique Center**
Route 202,
PA 18914 USA
Tel: 001 215 794 9180

Cheffins
Clifton House, 1&2
Clifton Road, Cambridge,
Cambridgeshire CB1 7EA
Tel: 01223 213 343
www.cheffins.co.uk

Chiswick Auctions
1–5 Colville Road,
London W3 8BL
Tel: 020 8992 4442
www.chiswickauctions.
co.uk

Colin Baddiel
351–3 Grays Antique
Market, 58 Davies Street,
London W1K 5LP
Tel: 020 7408 1239
Fax: 020 7493 9344

**Collectors Old Toy Shop
& Antiques**
89 Northgate, Halifax,
North Yorkshire, HX1 1XF
Tel: 01422 360 434

Dreweatt Neate
Donnington Priory
Salerooms, Donnington,
Newbury, Berkshire
RG14 2JE
Tel: 01635 553 553
www.dnfa.com/donnington

Fellows & Sons
Augusta House,
19 Augusta Street,
Hockley, Birmingham
B18 6JA

Tel: 0121 212 2131
info@fellows.co.uk
www.fellows.co.uk

Gorringes
15 North Street, Lewes,
East Sussex BN7 2PD
Tel: 01273 472 503
www.gorringes.co.uk

James D Julia Inc
PO Box 830, Fairfield,
ME 04937 USA
Tel: 001 207 453 7125
www.juliaauctions.com

**Kunst-Auktionshaus
Martin Wendl**
August-Bebel-Straße 4,
07407 Rudolstadt, Germany
Tel: 00 49 3672 4243 50
www.auktionshaus-
wendl.de

Lankes
Triftfeldstrasse 1,
95182 Döhlau, Germany
Tel: 0049 92 869 5050
www.lankes-auktionen.de

Litwin Antiques
PO Box 5865, Trenton,
NJ 08638 USA
Tel: 001 609 275 1427

Memory Lane
18 Rose Lane, Flowrtown,
PA 19031 USA
Tel: 001 215 233 4094
toyspost@aol.xom

Milezone's Toys
4025 South Franklin Street,
Michigan City, IN
46360 USA
Tel: 001 219 874 6629
sales@milezone.com
www.milezone.com

Neet-O-Rama
93 West Main Street,
Somerville, NJ 08876 USA
Tel: 001 908 722 4600
www.neetstuff.com

**Noel Barrett Antiques
& Auctions Ltd**
PO Box 300, Carversville,
PA 18913 USA
Tel: 001 215 297 5109
toys@noelbarrett.com
www.noelbarrett.com

**Philip Weiss
Auction Galleries**
1 Neil Court, Oceanside,
NY 11572 USA
Tel: 001 516 594 073
info@philipweissauctions.
com
www.philipweissauctions.
com

Sign of the Tymes
Mill Antiques Center,
12 Morris Farm Road,
Lafayette, NJ 07848 USA
Tel: 001 973 383 6028
jhap@nac.net
www.millantiques.com

Special Auction Services
Kennetholme, Midgham,
Nr. Reading, Berkshire,
RG7 5UX
Tel: 0118 971 2949
commemorative@aol.com
www.invaluable.com/sas

T.W. Conroy
36 Oswego Street,
Baldwinsville, NY 13027
Tel: 001 315 638 6434
Fax: 001 315 638 7039
www.twconroy.com

Thos. Wm. Gaze & Son
Diss Auction Rooms,
Roydon Road, Diss,
Norfolk IP22 4LN
Tel: 01379 650 306
www.twgaze.com

Vectis Auctions
Fleck Way, Thornaby,
Stockton on Tees, County
Durham TS17 9JZ
Tel: 01642 750 616
www.vectis.co.uk

**The Vintage Toy
& Train Shop**
Sidmouth Antiques
& Collectors Centre,
All Saint's Road, Sidmouth,
Exeter EX10 8ES
Tel: 01395 512 588

W.H. Peacock
26 Newham Street,
Bedford, MK40 3JR
Tel: 01234 266 366
Fax: 01234 269 082
info@peacockauction.co.uk
www.peacockauction.co,uk

Wallis and Wallis
West Street Auction
Galleries, Lewes, East
Sussex BN7 2NJ
Tel: 01273 480 208
www.wallisandwallis.co.uk

Wheels of Steel
Gray's Mews Antiques
Market, 58 Davies Street,
London W1Y 2LP
Woolley and Wallis
51–61 Castle Street,
Salisbury, Wiltshire
SP1 3SU
Tel: 01722 424 500
www.woolleyandwallis.
co.uk

COLLECTOR'S CLUBS

**The Antique Toy
Collectors of
America, Inc.**
c/o Carter, Ledyard &
Milburn, 2 Wall Street
(13th Floor), New York,
NY 10005 USA

Corgi Collector's Club
PO Box 323, Swansea,
Wales SA1 1BJ

Hornby Collector's Club
PO Box 35, Royston,
Hertfordshire SG8 5XR
Tel: 01223 208 308
hsclubs@demon.co.uk
www.hornby.co.uk

**The Matchbox® Toys
International Collector's
Association**
PO Box 120, Deeside,

Flintshire CH5 3HE
kevin@matchboxclub.com
www.matchboxclub.com

INDEX

PICTURE CREDITS

Auction Team Köln p.83; **Auktionhaus Kaup** p.10, p.13; **Bertoia Auctions** p.20, p.21, p.24, p.26, p.27, p.42, p.43, p.44, p.45, p.63, p.71, p.101, p.146, p.147, p.148, p.149, p.152, p.156, p.157, p.158, p.159, p.162, p.163, p.165, p.166, p.167, p.168, p.169, p.170, p.171, p.173, p.181, p.182, p.183, p.184, p.186, p.188, p.190, p.195, p.196, p.197, p.198, p.199, p.200, p.201, p.202, p.203, p.209, p.210, p.211, p.212, p.213, p.214, p.216, p.217, p.218, p.219, p.398, p.399, p.400, p.403; **Black Horse Antique Showcase** p.177, p.185; **Bucks County Antique Center** p.122, p.123; **Cheffins** p.33, p.58, p.63, p.117, p.125, p.126, p.226, p.227, p.247, p.254, p.289, p.291, p.326, p.405; **Chiswick Auctions** p.81; **Colin Baddiel** p.35, p.36, p.38,

p.41, p.53, p.98, p.130, p.237, p.246, p.253, p.255, p.256, p.257, p.288, p.315, p.326; **Dreweatt Neate** p.62, p.89, p.90, p.264, p.319; **Fellows & Sons** p.78, p.113; **Gorringes** p.111, **James D Julia** p.71; **Kunst-Auktionhaus Martin Wendl** p.100; **Lankes** p.12, p.20, p.25, p.27, p.59, p.85, p.86, p.87; **Neet-O-Rama** p.356, p.357, p.366, p.367, p.374, p.375, p.378, p.379, p.384, p.385; **Noel Barrett** p.24, p.56, p.57, p.58, p.66, p.68, p.70, p.73, p.74, p.75, p.76, p.77, p.145, p.150, p.172, p.180, p.187, p.189, p.204, p.208, p.215; **Private collection** p.65, p.175, p.177, p.178, p.191, p.192, p.193, p.402; **Philip Weiss** p.32, p.67, p.124, p.133, p.67; **Sign of the Tymes** p.354, p.358, p.359, p.360, p.360, p.361, p.363,

p.364, p.365, p.368, p.369, p.370, p.371, p.372, p.373, p.380, p.381, p.382, p.383, p.386, p.387 **Special Auction Services** p.416, p.422; **Thos. Wm. Gaze & Son** p.19, p.39, p.59, p.99, p.134, p.137, p.225, p.229, p.231, p.236, p.245, p.267, p.268, p.273, p.278, p.280, p.281, p.282, p.283, p.290, p.318, p.322, p.324, p.325, p.407, p.413, p.417, p.432, p.440; **T. W. Conroy** p.138; **Vectis Auctions** p.13, p.14, p.15, p.18, p.324, p.416, p.417, p.422, p.423, p.424, p.425, p.427, p.429, p.430, p.431, p.433, p.434, p.435, p.441; **Wallis and Wallis** p.19, p.22, p.23, p.25, p.30, p.31, p.46, p.47, p.49, p.50, p.52, p.54, p.55, p.68, p.77, p.78, p.79, p.95, p.97, p.99, p.103, p.104, p.105, p.106, p.107, p.108, p.109, p.110, p.112, p.115, p.116, p.120, p.121, p.127, p.128, p.129,

p.132, p.135, p.138, p.139, p.140, p.141, p.222, p.223, p.224, p.230, p.231, p.232, p.234, p.235, p.237, p.238, p.241, p.242, p.250, p.252, p.253, p.260, p.261, p.262, p.263, p.265, p.269, p.270, p.271, p.272, p.274, p.275, p.276, p.279, p.285, p.286, p.287, p.288, p.292, p.293, p.295, p.296, p.297, p.298, p.300, p.301, p.302, p.305, p.306, p.307, p.308, p.309, p.310, p.311, p.312, p.314, p.316, p.317, p.328, p.329, p.330, p.333, p.334, p.336, p.337, p.338, p.339, p.340, p.342, p.343, p.344, p.346, p.348, p.350, p.351, p.391, p.392, p.394, p.395, p.396, p.397, p.406, p.407, p.408, p.410, p.411, p.412, p.413, p.414, p.415, p.419, p.420, p.421, p.423, p.426, p.432, p.433, p.438, p.440; **W. H. Peacock** p.30, p.82, p.242, p.243, p.315, p.425; **Woolley and Wallis** p.96

ARCHIVE PICTURE ACKNOWLEDGMENTS

ACKNOWLEDGMENTS

AUTHOR'S ACKNOWLEDGMENTS

The Price Guide Company would like to thank the following for their contribution to the production of this book:

Photographers Graham Rae, Andy Johnson, and Byron Slater for their wonderful photography.

All of the dealers, auction houses, and private collectors for kindly allowing us to photograph their collections, particularly Bertoia Auctions, Chiswick Auctions, Colin Baddiel, Cheffins, Dreweatt Neate, Fellows & Sons, Gaze & Son, Gorringes, Noel Barrett, Neet-O-Rama, Peter Weiss Auction Galleries, Special Auction Services, Sign of the Tymes, Auction Team Köln, TW Conroy, Vectis Auctions, Wallis & Wallis, and Woolley & Wallis.

Also special thanks to Jessica Bishop, Dan Dunlavey, Mark Hill, Sandra Lange, Cathy Marriott, Claire Smith, and Sara Sturgess for their editorial contribution and help with image sourcing.

Thanks also to Digital Image Co-ordinator Ellen Sinclair and Workflow Consultant Bob Bousfield.

PUBLISHER'S ACKNOWLEDGMENTS

Dorling Kindersley would like to thank the following for their contribution to the production of this book:

Sarah Smithies for picture research, Sara Sha'ath for proofreading, Tamsin Curtis for proofreading and co-ordinating proofs, Dawn Henderson and Kathryn Wilkinson for additional editorial help, and Hilary Bird for indexing.

MANUFACTURER'S NOTE